Childe Harold's Pilgrimage

Childe Harold's Pilgrimage

Lord Byron

MINT EDITIONS

Childe Harold's Pilgrimage was first published in 1812.

This edition published by Mint Editions 2021.

ISBN 9781513268866 | E-ISBN 9781513273860

Published by Mint Editions®

 MINT
EDITIONS

minteditionbooks.com

Publishing Director: Jennifer Newens
Design & Production: Rachel Lopez Metzger
Typesetting: Westchester Publishing Services

Contents

To Ianthe

Not in those climes where I have late been straying,
    Though Beauty long hath there been matchless deemed,
Not in those visions to the heart displaying
    Forms which it sighs but to have only dreamed,
    Hath aught like thee in truth or fancy seemed:
Nor, having seen thee, shall I vainly seek
    To paint those charms which varied as they beamed—
    To such as see thee not my words were weak;
To those who gaze on thee, what language could they speak?

Ah! mayst thou ever be what now thou art,
    Nor unbeseem the promise of thy spring,
As fair in form, as warm yet pure in heart,
    Love's image upon earth without his wing,
    And guileless beyond Hope's imagining!
And surely she who now so fondly rears
    Thy youth, in thee, thus hourly brightening,
    Beholds the rainbow of her future years,
Before whose heavenly hues all sorrow disappears.

Young Peri of the West!—'tis well for me
    My years already doubly number thine;
My loveless eye unmoved may gaze on thee,
    And safely view thy ripening beauties shine:
    Happy, I ne'er shall see them in decline;
Happier, that while all younger hearts shall bleed
    Mine shall escape the doom thine eyes assign
    To those whose admiration shall succeed,
But mixed with pangs to Love's even loveliest hours decreed.

Oh! let that eye, which, wild as the gazelle's,
    Now brightly bold or beautifully shy,
Wins as it wanders, dazzles where it dwells,
    Glance o'er this page, nor to my verse deny
    That smile for which my breast might vainly sigh,
Could I to thee be ever more than friend:

This much, dear maid, accord; nor question why
To one so young my strain I would commend,
But bid me with my wreath one matchless lily blend.

Such is thy name with this my verse entwined;
And long as kinder eyes a look shall cast
On Harold's page, Ianthe's here enshrined
Shall thus be first beheld, forgotten last:
My days once numbered, should this homage past
Attract thy fairy fingers near the lyre
Of him who hailed thee, loveliest as thou wast,
Such is the most my memory may desire;
Though more than Hope can claim, could Friendship less require?

LORD BYRON

Canto the First

I

Oh, thou, in Hellas deemed of heavenly birth,
Muse, formed or fabled at the minstrel's will!
Since shamed full oft by later lyres on earth,
Mine dares not call thee from thy sacred hill:
Yet there I've wandered by thy vaunted rill;
Yes! sighed o'er Delphi's long-deserted shrine
Where, save that feeble fountain, all is still;
Nor mote my shell awake the weary Nine
To grace so plain a tale—this lowly lay of mine.

II

Whilome in Albion's isle there dwelt a youth,
Who ne in virtue's ways did take delight;
But spent his days in riot most uncouth,
And vexed with mirth the drowsy ear of Night.
Ah, me! in sooth he was a shameless wight,
Sore given to revel and ungodly glee;
Few earthly things found favour in his sight
Save concubines and carnal companie,
And flaunting wassailers of high and low degree.

III

Childe Harold was he hight:—but whence his name
And lineage long, it suits me not to say;
Suffice it, that perchance they were of fame,
And had been glorious in another day:
But one sad losel soils a name for aye,
However mighty in the olden time;
Nor all that heralds rake from coffined clay,
Nor florid prose, nor honeyed lines of rhyme,
Can blazon evil deeds, or consecrate a crime.

IV

Childe Harold basked him in the noontide sun,
Disporting there like any other fly,
Nor deemed before his little day was done
One blast might chill him into misery.
But long ere scarce a third of his passed by,
Worse than adversity the Childe befell;
He felt the fulness of satiety:
Then loathed he in his native land to dwell,
Which seemed to him more lone than eremite's sad cell.

V

For he through Sin's long labyrinth had run,
Nor made atonement when he did amiss,
Had sighed to many, though he loved but one,
And that loved one, alas, could ne'er be his.
Ah, happy she! to 'scape from him whose kiss
Had been pollution unto aught so chaste;
Who soon had left her charms for vulgar bliss,
And spoiled her goodly lands to gild his waste,
Nor calm domestic peace had ever deigned to taste.

VI

And now Childe Harold was sore sick at heart,
And from his fellow bacchanals would flee;
'Tis said, at times the sullen tear would start,
But pride congealed the drop within his e'e:
Apart he stalked in joyless reverie,
And from his native land resolved to go,
And visit scorching climes beyond the sea;
With pleasure drugged, he almost longed for woe,
And e'en for change of scene would seek the shades below.

VII

The Childe departed from his father's hall;
It was a vast and venerable pile;
So old, it seemed only not to fall,
Yet strength was pillared in each massy aisle.
Monastic dome! condemned to uses vile!
Where superstition once had made her den,
Now Paphian girls were known to sing and smile;
And monks might deem their time was come agen,
If ancient tales say true, nor wrong these holy men.

VIII

Yet ofttimes in his maddest mirthful mood,
Strange pangs would flash along Childe Harold's brow,
As if the memory of some deadly feud
Or disappointed passion lurked below:
But this none knew, nor haply cared to know;
For his was not that open, artless soul
That feels relief by bidding sorrow flow;
Nor sought he friend to counsel or condole,
Whate'er this grief mote be, which he could not control.

IX

And none did love him: though to hall and bower
He gathered revellers from far and near,
He knew them flatterers of the festal hour;
The heartless parasites of present cheer.
Yea, none did love him—not his lemans dear—
But pomp and power alone are woman's care,
And where these are light Eros finds a feere;
Maidens, like moths, are ever caught by glare,
And Mammon wins his way where seraphs might despair.

X

Childe Harold had a mother—not forgot,
Though parting from that mother he did shun;
A sister whom he loved, but saw her not
Before his weary pilgrimage begun:
If friends he had, he bade adieu to none.
Yet deem not thence his breast a breast of steel;
Ye, who have known what 'tis to dote upon
A few dear objects, will in sadness feel
Such partings break the heart they fondly hope to heal.

XI

His house, his home, his heritage, his lands,
The laughing dames in whom he did delight,
Whose large blue eyes, fair locks, and snowy hands,
Might shake the saintship of an anchorite,
And long had fed his youthful appetite;
His goblets brimmed with every costly wine,
And all that mote to luxury invite,
Without a sigh he left to cross the brine,
And traverse Paynim shores, and pass earth's central line.

XII

The sails were filled, and fair the light winds blew
As glad to waft him from his native home;
And fast the white rocks faded from his view,
And soon were lost in circumambient foam;
And then, it may be, of his wish to roam
Repented he, but in his bosom slept
The silent thought, nor from his lips did come
One word of wail, whilst others sate and wept,
And to the reckless gales unmanly moaning kept.

LORD BYRON

XIII

But when the sun was sinking in the sea,
He seized his harp, which he at times could string,
And strike, albeit with untaught melody,
When deemed he no strange ear was listening:
And now his fingers o'er it he did fling,
And tuned his farewell in the dim twilight,
While flew the vessel on her snowy wing,
And fleeting shores receded from his sight,
Thus to the elements he poured his last 'Good Night.'

Adieu, adieu! my native shore
    Fades o'er the waters blue;
The night-winds sigh, the breakers roar,
    And shrieks the wild sea-mew.
Yon sun that sets upon the sea
    We follow in his flight;
Farewell awhile to him and thee,
    My Native Land—Good Night!

A few short hours, and he will rise
    To give the morrow birth;
And I shall hail the main and skies,
    But not my mother earth.
Deserted is my own good hall,
    Its hearth is desolate;
Wild weeds are gathering on the wall,
    My dog howls at the gate.

'Come hither, hither, my little page:
    Why dost thou weep and wail?
Or dost thou dread the billow's rage,
    Or tremble at the gale?
But dash the tear-drop from thine eye,
    Our ship is swift and strong;
Our fleetest falcon scarce can fly
    More merrily along.'

'Let winds be shrill, let waves roll high,
    I fear not wave nor wind;
Yet marvel not, Sir Childe, that I
    Am sorrowful in mind;
For I have from my father gone,
    A mother whom I love,
And have no friend, save these alone,
    But thee—and One above.

'My father blessed me fervently,
    Yet did not much complain;
But sorely will my mother sigh
    Till I come back again.'—
'Enough, enough, my little lad!
    Such tears become thine eye;
If I thy guileless bosom had,
    Mine own would not be dry.

'Come hither, hither, my staunch yeoman,
    Why dost thou look so pale?
Or dost thou dread a French foeman,
    Or shiver at the gale?'—
'Deem'st thou I tremble for my life?
    Sir Childe, I'm not so weak;
But thinking on an absent wife
    Will blanch a faithful cheek.

'My spouse and boys dwell near thy hall,
    Along the bordering lake;
And when they on their father call,
    What answer shall she make?'—
'Enough, enough, my yeoman good,
    Thy grief let none gainsay;
But I, who am of lighter mood,
    Will laugh to flee away.'

For who would trust the seeming sighs
    Of wife or paramour?

Fresh feeres will dry the bright blue eyes
    We late saw streaming o'er.
For pleasures past I do not grieve,
    Nor perils gathering near;
My greatest grief is that I leave
    No thing that claims a tear.

And now I'm in the world alone,
    Upon the wide, wide sea;
But why should I for others groan,
    When none will sigh for me?
Perchance my dog will whine in vain
    Till fed by stranger hands;
But long ere I come back again
    He'd tear me where he stands.

With thee, my bark, I'll swiftly go
    Athwart the foaming brine;
Nor care what land thou bear'st me to,
    So not again to mine.
Welcome, welcome, ye dark blue waves!
    And when you fail my sight,
Welcome, ye deserts, and ye caves!
    My Native Land—Good Night!

XIV

On, on the vessel flies, the land is gone,
And winds are rude in Biscay's sleepless bay.
Four days are sped, but with the fifth, anon,
New shores descried make every bosom gay;
And Cintra's mountain greets them on their way,
And Tagus dashing onward to the deep,
His fabled golden tribute bent to pay;
And soon on board the Lusian pilots leap,
And steer 'twixt fertile shores where yet few rustics reap.

XV

Oh, Christ! it is a goodly sight to see
What Heaven hath done for this delicious land!
What fruits of fragrance blush on every tree!
What goodly prospects o'er the hills expand!
But man would mar them with an impious hand:
And when the Almighty lifts his fiercest scourge
'Gainst those who most transgress his high command,
With treble vengeance will his hot shafts urge
Gaul's locust host, and earth from fellest foemen purge.

XVI

What beauties doth Lisboa first unfold!
Her image floating on that noble tide,
Which poets vainly pave with sands of gold,
But now whereon a thousand keels did ride
Of mighty strength, since Albion was allied,
And to the Lusians did her aid afford
A nation swoll'n with ignorance and pride,
Who lick, yet loathe, the hand that waves the sword.
To save them from the wrath of Gaul's unsparing lord.

XVII

But whoso entereth within this town,
That, sheening far, celestial seems to be,
Disconsolate will wander up and down,
Mid many things unsightly to strange e'e;
For hut and palace show like filthily;
The dingy denizens are reared in dirt;
No personage of high or mean degree
Doth care for cleanness of surtout or shirt,
Though shent with Egypt's plague, unkempt, unwashed, unhurt.

LORD BYRON

XVIII

Poor, paltry slaves! yet born midst noblest scenes—
Why, Nature, waste thy wonders on such men?
Lo! Cintra's glorious Eden intervenes
In variegated maze of mount and glen.
Ah me! what hand can pencil guide, or pen,
To follow half on which the eye dilates
Through views more dazzling unto mortal ken
Than those whereof such things the bard relates,
Who to the awe-struck world unlocked Elysium's gates?

XIX

The horrid crags, by toppling convent crowned,
The cork-trees hoar that clothe the shaggy steep,
The mountain moss by scorching skies imbrowned,
The sunken glen, whose sunless shrubs must weep,
The tender azure of the unruffled deep,
The orange tints that gild the greenest bough,
The torrents that from cliff to valley leap,
The vine on high, the willow branch below,
Mixed in one mighty scene, with varied beauty glow.

XX

Then slowly climb the many-winding way,
And frequent turn to linger as you go,
From loftier rocks new loveliness survey,
And rest ye at 'Our Lady's House of Woe;'
Where frugal monks their little relics show,
And sundry legends to the stranger tell:
Here impious men have punished been; and lo,
Deep in yon cave Honorius long did dwell,
In hope to merit Heaven by making earth a Hell.

XXI

And here and there, as up the crags you spring,
Mark many rude-carved crosses near the path;
Yet deem not these devotion's offering—
These are memorials frail of murderous wrath;
For wheresoe'er the shrieking victim hath
Poured forth his blood beneath the assassin's knife,
Some hand erects a cross of mouldering lath;
And grove and glen with thousand such are rife
Throughout this purple land, where law secures not life!

XXII

On sloping mounds, or in the vale beneath,
Are domes where whilom kings did make repair;
But now the wild flowers round them only breathe:
Yet ruined splendour still is lingering there.
And yonder towers the prince's palace fair:
There thou, too, Vathek! England's wealthiest son,
Once formed thy Paradise, as not aware
When wanton Wealth her mightiest deeds hath done,
Meek Peace voluptuous lures was ever wont to shun.

XXIII

Here didst thou dwell, here schemes of pleasure plan.
Beneath yon mountain's ever beauteous brow;
But now, as if a thing unblest by man,
Thy fairy dwelling is as lone as thou!
Here giant weeds a passage scarce allow
To halls deserted, portals gaping wide;
Fresh lessons to the thinking bosom, how
Vain are the pleasaunces on earth supplied;
Swept into wrecks anon by Time's ungentle tide.

XXIV

Behold the hall where chiefs were late convened!
Oh! dome displeasing unto British eye!
With diadem hight foolscap, lo! a fiend,
A little fiend that scoffs incessantly,
There sits in parchment robe arrayed, and by
His side is hung a seal and sable scroll,
Where blazoned glare names known to chivalry,
And sundry signatures adorn the roll,
Whereat the urchin points, and laughs with all his soul.

XXV

Convention is the dwarfish demon styled
That foiled the knights in Marialva's dome:
Of brains (if brains they had) he them beguiled,
And turned a nation's shallow joy to gloom.
Here Folly dashed to earth the victor's plume,
And Policy regained what Arms had lost:
For chiefs like ours in vain may laurels bloom!
Woe to the conquering, not the conquered host,
Since baffled Triumph droops on Lusitania's coast.

XXVI

And ever since that martial synod met,
Britannia sickens, Cintra, at thy name;
And folks in office at the mention fret,
And fain would blush, if blush they could, for shame.
How will posterity the deed proclaim!
Will not our own and fellow-nations sneer,
To view these champions cheated of their fame,
By foes in fight o'erthrown, yet victors here,
Where Scorn her finger points through many a coming year?

XXVII

So deemed the Childe, as o'er the mountains he
Did take his way in solitary guise:
Sweet was the scene, yet soon he thought to flee,
More restless than the swallow in the skies:
Though here awhile he learned to moralise,
For Meditation fixed at times on him,
And conscious Reason whispered to despise
His early youth misspent in maddest whim;
But as he gazed on Truth, his aching eyes grew dim.

XXVIII

To horse! to horse! he quits, for ever quits
A scene of peace, though soothing to his soul:
Again he rouses from his moping fits,
But seeks not now the harlot and the bowl.
Onward he flies, nor fixed as yet the goal
Where he shall rest him on his pilgrimage;
And o'er him many changing scenes must roll,
Ere toil his thirst for travel can assuage,
Or he shall calm his breast, or learn experience sage.

XXIX

Yet Mafra shall one moment claim delay,
Where dwelt of yore the Lusians' luckless queen;
And church and court did mingle their array,
And mass and revel were alternate seen;
Lordlings and freres—ill-sorted fry, I ween!
But here the Babylonian whore had built
A dome, where flaunts she in such glorious sheen,
That men forget the blood which she hath spilt,
And bow the knee to Pomp that loves to garnish guilt.

XXX

O'er vales that teem with fruits, romantic hills,
(Oh that such hills upheld a free-born race!)
Whereon to gaze the eye with joyaunce fills,
Childe Harold wends through many a pleasant place.
Though sluggards deem it but a foolish chase,
And marvel men should quit their easy chair,
The toilsome way, and long, long league to trace.
Oh, there is sweetness in the mountain air
And life, that bloated Ease can never hope to share.

XXXI

More bleak to view the hills at length recede,
And, less luxuriant, smoother vales extend:
Immense horizon-bounded plains succeed!
Far as the eye discerns, withouten end,
Spain's realms appear, whereon her shepherds tend
Flocks, whose rich fleece right well the trader knows—
Now must the pastor's arm his lambs defend:
For Spain is compassed by unyielding foes,
And all must shield their all, or share Subjection's woes.

XXXII

Where Lusitania and her Sister meet,
Deem ye what bounds the rival realms divide?
Or e'er the jealous queens of nations greet,
Doth Tayo interpose his mighty tide?
Or dark sierras rise in craggy pride?
Or fence of art, like China's vasty wall?—
Ne barrier wall, ne river deep and wide,
Ne horrid crags, nor mountains dark and tall
Rise like the rocks that part Hispania's land from Gaul

XXXIII

But these between a silver streamlet glides,
And scarce a name distinguisheth the brook,
Though rival kingdoms press its verdant sides.
Here leans the idle shepherd on his crook,
And vacant on the rippling waves doth look,
That peaceful still 'twixt bitterest foemen flow:
For proud each peasant as the noblest duke:
Well doth the Spanish hind the difference know
'Twixt him and Lusian slave, the lowest of the low.

XXXIV

But ere the mingling bounds have far been passed,
Dark Guadiana rolls his power along
In sullen billows, murmuring and vast,
So noted ancient roundelays among.
Whilome upon his banks did legions throng
Of Moor and Knight, in mailed splendour drest;
Here ceased the swift their race, here sunk the strong;
The Paynim turban and the Christian crest
Mixed on the bleeding stream, by floating hosts oppressed.

XXXV

Oh, lovely Spain! renowned, romantic land!
Where is that standard which Pelagio bore,
When Cava's traitor-sire first called the band
That dyed thy mountain-streams with Gothic gore?
Where are those bloody banners which of yore
Waved o'er thy sons, victorious to the gale,
And drove at last the spoilers to their shore?
Red gleamed the cross, and waned the crescent pale,
While Afric's echoes thrilled with Moorish matrons' wail.

XXXVI

Teems not each ditty with the glorious tale?
Ah! such, alas, the hero's amplest fate!
When granite moulders and when records fail,
A peasant's plaint prolongs his dubious date.
Pride! bend thine eye from heaven to thine estate,
See how the mighty shrink into a song!
Can volume, pillar, pile, preserve thee great?
Or must thou trust Tradition's simple tongue,
When Flattery sleeps with thee, and History does thee wrong?

XXXVII

Awake, ye sons of Spain! awake! advance
Lo! Chivalry, your ancient goddess, cries,
But wields not, as of old, her thirsty lance,
Nor shakes her crimson plumage in the skies:
Now on the smoke of blazing bolts she flies,
And speaks in thunder through yon engine's roar!
In every peal she calls—'Awake! arise!'
Say, is her voice more feeble than of yore,
When her war-song was heard on Andalusia's shore?

XXXVIII

Hark! heard you not those hoofs of dreadful note?
Sounds not the clang of conflict on the heath?
Saw ye not whom the reeking sabre smote;
Nor saved your brethren ere they sank beneath
Tyrants and tyrants' slaves?—the fires of death,
The bale-fires flash on high:—from rock to rock
Each volley tells that thousands cease to breathe:
Death rides upon the sulphury Siroc,
Red Battle stamps his foot, and nations feel the shock.

XXXIX

Lo! where the Giant on the mountain stands,
His blood-red tresses deepening in the sun,
With death-shot glowing in his fiery hands,
And eye that scorcheth all it glares upon;
Restless it rolls, now fixed, and now anon
Flashing afar,—and at his iron feet
Destruction cowers, to mark what deeds are done;
For on this morn three potent nations meet,
To shed before his shrine the blood he deems most sweet.

XL

By Heaven! it is a splendid sight to see
(For one who hath no friend, no brother there)
Their rival scarfs of mixed embroidery,
Their various arms that glitter in the air!
What gallant war-hounds rouse them from their lair,
And gnash their fangs, loud yelling for the prey!
All join the chase, but few the triumph share:
The Grave shall bear the chiefest prize away,
And Havoc scarce for joy can cumber their array.

XLI

Three hosts combine to offer sacrifice;
Three tongues prefer strange orisons on high;
Three gaudy standards flout the pale blue skies.
The shouts are France, Spain, Albion, Victory!
The foe, the victim, and the fond ally
That fights for all, but ever fights in vain,
Are met—as if at home they could not die—
To feed the crow on Talavera's plain,
And fertilise the field that each pretends to gain.

XLII

There shall they rot—Ambition's honoured fools!
Yes, Honour decks the turf that wraps their clay!
Vain Sophistry! in these behold the tools,
The broken tools, that tyrants cast away
By myriads, when they dare to pave their way
With human hearts—to what?—a dream alone.
Can despots compass aught that hails their sway?
Or call with truth one span of earth their own,
Save that wherein at last they crumble bone by bone?

XLIII

O Albuera, glorious field of grief!
As o'er thy plain the Pilgrim pricked his steed,
Who could foresee thee, in a space so brief,
A scene where mingling foes should boast and bleed.
Peace to the perished! may the warrior's meed
And tears of triumph their reward prolong!
Till others fall where other chieftains lead,
Thy name shall circle round the gaping throng,
And shine in worthless lays, the theme of transient song.

XLIV

Enough of Battle's minions! let them play
Their game of lives, and barter breath for fame:
Fame that will scarce reanimate their clay,
Though thousands fall to deck some single name.
In sooth, 'twere sad to thwart their noble aim
Who strike, blest hirelings! for their country's good,
And die, that living might have proved her shame;
Perished, perchance, in some domestic feud,
Or in a narrower sphere wild Rapine's path pursued.

XLV

Full swiftly Harold wends his lonely way
Where proud Sevilla triumphs unsubdued:
Yet is she free—the spoiler's wished-for prey!
Soon, soon shall Conquest's fiery foot intrude,
Blackening her lovely domes with traces rude.
Inevitable hour! 'Gainst fate to strive
Where Desolation plants her famished brood
Is vain, or Ilion, Tyre, might yet survive,
And Virtue vanquish all, and Murder cease to thrive.

XLVI

But all unconscious of the coming doom,
The feast, the song, the revel here abounds;
Strange modes of merriment the hours consume,
Nor bleed these patriots with their country's wounds;
Nor here War's clarion, but Love's rebeck sounds;
Here Folly still his votaries enthralls,
And young-eyed Lewdness walks her midnight rounds:
Girt with the silent crimes of capitals,
Still to the last kind Vice clings to the tottering walls.

XLVII

Not so the rustic: with his trembling mate
He lurks, nor casts his heavy eye afar,
Lest he should view his vineyard desolate,
Blasted below the dun hot breath of war.
No more beneath soft Eve's consenting star
Fandango twirls his jocund castanet:
Ah, monarchs! could ye taste the mirth ye mar,
Not in the toils of Glory would ye fret;
The hoarse dull drum would sleep, and Man be happy yet.

XLVIII

How carols now the lusty muleteer?
Of love, romance, devotion is his lay,
As whilome he was wont the leagues to cheer,
His quick bells wildly jingling on the way?
No! as he speeds, he chants 'Viva el Rey!'
And checks his song to execrate Godoy,
The royal wittol Charles, and curse the day
When first Spain's queen beheld the black-eyed boy,
And gore-faced Treason sprung from her adulterate joy.

XLIX

On yon long level plain, at distance crowned
With crags, whereon those Moorish turrets rest,
Wide scattered hoof-marks dint the wounded ground;
And, scathed by fire, the greensward's darkened vest
Tells that the foe was Andalusia's guest:
Here was the camp, the watch-flame, and the host,
Here the brave peasant stormed the dragon's nest;
Still does he mark it with triumphant boast,
And points to yonder cliffs, which oft were won and lost.

L

And whomsoe'er along the path you meet
Bears in his cap the badge of crimson hue,
Which tells you whom to shun and whom to greet:
Woe to the man that walks in public view
Without of loyalty this token true:
Sharp is the knife, and sudden is the stroke;
And sorely would the Gallic foemen rue,
If subtle poniards, wrapt beneath the cloak,
Could blunt the sabre's edge, or clear the cannon's smoke.

LI

At every turn Morena's dusky height
Sustains aloft the battery's iron load;
And, far as mortal eye can compass sight,
The mountain-howitzer, the broken road,
The bristling palisade, the fosse o'erflowed,
The stationed bands, the never-vacant watch,
The magazine in rocky durance stowed,
The holstered steed beneath the shed of thatch,
The ball-piled pyramid, the ever-blazing match,

LII

Portend the deeds to come:—but he whose nod
Has tumbled feebler despots from their sway,
A moment pauseth ere he lifts the rod;
A little moment deigneth to delay:
Soon will his legions sweep through these the way;
The West must own the Scourger of the world.
Ah, Spain! how sad will be thy reckoning day,
When soars Gaul's Vulture, with his wings unfurled,
And thou shalt view thy sons in crowds to Hades hurled.

LIII

And must they fall—the young, the proud, the brave—
To swell one bloated chief's unwholesome reign?
No step between submission and a grave?
The rise of rapine and the fall of Spain?
And doth the Power that man adores ordain
Their doom, nor heed the suppliant's appeal?
Is all that desperate Valour acts in vain?
And Counsel sage, and patriotic Zeal,
The veteran's skill, youth's fire, and manhood's heart of steel?

LIV

Is it for this the Spanish maid, aroused,
Hangs on the willow her unstrung guitar,
And, all unsexed, the anlace hath espoused,
Sung the loud song, and dared the deed of war?
And she, whom once the semblance of a scar
Appalled, an owlet's larum chilled with dread,
Now views the column-scattering bayonet jar,
The falchion flash, and o'er the yet warm dead
Stalks with Minerva's step where Mars might quake to tread.

LV

Ye who shall marvel when you hear her tale,
Oh! had you known her in her softer hour,
Marked her black eye that mocks her coal-black veil,
Heard her light, lively tones in lady's bower,
Seen her long locks that foil the painter's power,
Her fairy form, with more than female grace,
Scarce would you deem that Saragoza's tower
Beheld her smile in Danger's Gorgon face,
Thin the closed ranks, and lead in Glory's fearful chase.

LVI

Her lover sinks—she sheds no ill-timed tear;
Her chief is slain—she fills his fatal post;
Her fellows flee—she checks their base career;
The foe retires—she heads the sallying host:
Who can appease like her a lover's ghost?
Who can avenge so well a leader's fall?
What maid retrieve when man's flushed hope is lost?
Who hang so fiercely on the flying Gaul,
Foiled by a woman's hand, before a battered wall?

LVII

Yet are Spain's maids no race of Amazons,
But formed for all the witching arts of love:
Though thus in arms they emulate her sons,
And in the horrid phalanx dare to move,
'Tis but the tender fierceness of the dove,
Pecking the hand that hovers o'er her mate:
In softness as in firmness far above
Remoter females, famed for sickening prate;
Her mind is nobler sure, her charms perchance as great.

LVIII

The seal Love's dimpling finger hath impressed
Denotes how soft that chin which bears his touch:
Her lips, whose kisses pout to leave their nest,
Bid man be valiant ere he merit such:
Her glance, how wildly beautiful! how much
Hath Phoebus wooed in vain to spoil her cheek
Which glows yet smoother from his amorous clutch!
Who round the North for paler dames would seek?
How poor their forms appear? how languid, wan, and weak!

LIX

Match me, ye climes! which poets love to laud;
Match me, ye harems! of the land where now
I strike my strain, far distant, to applaud
Beauties that even a cynic must avow!
Match me those houris, whom ye scarce allow
To taste the gale lest Love should ride the wind,
With Spain's dark-glancing daughters—deign to know,
There your wise Prophet's paradise we find,
His black-eyed maids of Heaven, angelically kind.

LX

O thou, Parnassus! whom I now survey,
Not in the frenzy of a dreamer's eye,
Not in the fabled landscape of a lay,
But soaring snow-clad through thy native sky,
In the wild pomp of mountain majesty!
What marvel if I thus essay to sing?
The humblest of thy pilgrims passing by
Would gladly woo thine echoes with his string,
Though from thy heights no more one muse will wave her wing.

LXI

Oft have I dreamed of thee! whose glorious name
Who knows not, knows not man's divinest lore:
And now I view thee, 'tis, alas, with shame
That I in feeblest accents must adore.
When I recount thy worshippers of yore
I tremble, and can only bend the knee;
Nor raise my voice, nor vainly dare to soar,
But gaze beneath thy cloudy canopy
In silent joy to think at last I look on thee!

LXII

Happier in this than mightiest bards have been,
Whose fate to distant homes confined their lot,
Shall I unmoved behold the hallowed scene,
Which others rave of, though they know it not?
Though here no more Apollo haunts his grot,
And thou, the Muses' seat, art now their grave,
Some gentle spirit still pervades the spot,
Sighs in the gale, keeps silence in the cave,
And glides with glassy foot o'er yon melodious wave.

LXIII

Of thee hereafter.—Even amidst my strain
I turned aside to pay my homage here;
Forgot the land, the sons, the maids of Spain;
Her fate, to every free-born bosom dear;
And hailed thee, not perchance without a tear.
Now to my theme—but from thy holy haunt
Let me some remnant, some memorial bear;
Yield me one leaf of Daphne's deathless plant,
Nor let thy votary's hope be deemed an idle vaunt.

LXIV

But ne'er didst thou, fair mount, when Greece was young,
See round thy giant base a brighter choir;
Nor e'er did Delphi, when her priestess sung
The Pythian hymn with more than mortal fire,
Behold a train more fitting to inspire
The song of love than Andalusia's maids,
Nurst in the glowing lap of soft desire:
Ah! that to these were given such peaceful shades
As Greece can still bestow, though Glory fly her glades.

LXV

Fair is proud Seville; let her country boast
Her strength, her wealth, her site of ancient days,
But Cadiz, rising on the distant coast,
Calls forth a sweeter, though ignoble praise.
Ah, Vice! how soft are thy voluptuous ways!
While boyish blood is mantling, who can 'scape
The fascination of thy magic gaze?
A cherub-hydra round us dost thou gape,
And mould to every taste thy dear delusive shape.

LXVI

When Paphos fell by Time—accursed Time!
The Queen who conquers all must yield to thee—
The Pleasures fled, but sought as warm a clime;
And Venus, constant to her native sea,
To nought else constant, hither deigned to flee,
And fixed her shrine within these walls of white;
Though not to one dome circumscribeth she
Her worship, but, devoted to her rite,
A thousand altars rise, for ever blazing bright.

LXVII

From morn till night, from night till startled morn
Peeps blushing on the revel's laughing crew,
The song is heard, the rosy garland worn;
Devices quaint, and frolics ever new,
Tread on each other's kibes. A long adieu
He bids to sober joy that here sojourns:
Nought interrupts the riot, though in lieu
Of true devotion monkish incense burns,
And love and prayer unite, or rule the hour by turns.

LXVIII

The sabbath comes, a day of blessed rest;
What hallows it upon this Christian shore?
Lo! it is sacred to a solemn feast:
Hark! heard you not the forest monarch's roar?
Crashing the lance, he snuffs the spouting gore
Of man and steed, o'erthrown beneath his horn:
The thronged arena shakes with shouts for more;
Yells the mad crowd o'er entrails freshly torn,
Nor shrinks the female eye, nor e'en affects to mourn.

LXIX

The seventh day this; the jubilee of man.
London! right well thou know'st the day of prayer:
Then thy spruce citizen, washed artizan,
And smug apprentice gulp their weekly air:
Thy coach of hackney, whiskey, one-horse chair,
And humblest gig, through sundry suburbs whirl;
To Hampstead, Brentford, Harrow, make repair;
Till the tired jade the wheel forgets to hurl,
Provoking envious gibe from each pedestrian churl.

LXX

Some o'er thy Thamis row the ribboned fair,
Others along the safer turnpike fly;
Some Richmond Hill ascend, some scud to Ware,
And many to the steep of Highgate hie.
Ask ye, Boeotian shades, the reason why?
'Tis to the worship of the solemn Horn,
Grasped in the holy hand of Mystery,
In whose dread name both men and maids are sworn,
And consecrate the oath with draught and dance till morn.

LXXI

All have their fooleries; not alike are thine,
Fair Cadiz, rising o'er the dark blue sea!
Soon as the matin bell proclaimeth nine,
Thy saint adorers count the rosary:
Much is the Virgin teased to shrive them free
(Well do I ween the only virgin there)
From crimes as numerous as her beadsmen be;
Then to the crowded circus forth they fare:
Young, old, high, low, at once the same diversion share.

LXXII

The lists are oped, the spacious area cleared,
Thousands on thousands piled are seated round;
Long ere the first loud trumpet's note is heard,
No vacant space for lated wight is found:
Here dons, grandees, but chiefly dames abound,
Skilled in the ogle of a roguish eye,
Yet ever well inclined to heal the wound;
None through their cold disdain are doomed to die,
As moon-struck bards complain, by Love's sad archery.

LXXIII

Hushed is the din of tongues—on gallant steeds,
With milk-white crest, gold spur, and light-poised lance,
Four cavaliers prepare for venturous deeds,
And lowly bending to the lists advance;
Rich are their scarfs, their chargers featly prance:
If in the dangerous game they shine to-day,
The crowd's loud shout, and ladies' lovely glance,
Best prize of better acts, they bear away,
And all that kings or chiefs e'er gain their toils repay.

LXXIV

In costly sheen and gaudy cloak arrayed,
But all afoot, the light-limbed matadore
Stands in the centre, eager to invade
The lord of lowing herds; but not before
The ground, with cautious tread, is traversed o'er,
Lest aught unseen should lurk to thwart his speed:
His arms a dart, he fights aloof, nor more
Can man achieve without the friendly steed—
Alas! too oft condemned for him to bear and bleed.

LXXV

Thrice sounds the clarion; lo! the signal falls,
The den expands, and expectation mute
Gapes round the silent circle's peopled walls.
Bounds with one lashing spring the mighty brute,
And wildly staring, spurns, with sounding foot,
The sand, nor blindly rushes on his foe:
Here, there, he points his threatening front, to suit
His first attack, wide waving to and fro
His angry tail; red rolls his eye's dilated glow.

LXXVI

Sudden he stops; his eye is fixed: away,
Away, thou heedless boy! prepare the spear;
Now is thy time to perish, or display
The skill that yet may check his mad career.
With well-timed croupe the nimble coursers veer;
On foams the bull, but not unscathed he goes;
Streams from his flank the crimson torrent clear:
He flies, he wheels, distracted with his throes:
Dart follows dart; lance, lance; loud bellowings speak his woes.

LXXVII

Again he comes; nor dart nor lance avail,
Nor the wild plunging of the tortured horse;
Though man and man's avenging arms assail,
Vain are his weapons, vainer is his force.
One gallant steed is stretched a mangled corse;
Another, hideous sight! unseamed appears,
His gory chest unveils life's panting source;
Though death-struck, still his feeble frame he rears;
Staggering, but stemming all, his lord unharmed he bears.

LXXVIII

Foiled, bleeding, breathless, furious to the last,
Full in the centre stands the bull at bay,
Mid wounds, and clinging darts, and lances brast,
And foes disabled in the brutal fray:
And now the matadores around him play,
Shake the red cloak, and poise the ready brand:
Once more through all he bursts his thundering way—
Vain rage! the mantle quits the conynge hand,
Wraps his fierce eye—'tis past—he sinks upon the sand.

LXXIX

Where his vast neck just mingles with the spine,
Sheathed in his form the deadly weapon lies.
He stops—he starts—disdaining to decline:
Slowly he falls, amidst triumphant cries,
Without a groan, without a struggle dies.
The decorated car appears on high:
The corse is piled—sweet sight for vulgar eyes;
Four steeds that spurn the rein, as swift as shy,
Hurl the dark bull along, scarce seen in dashing by.

LXXX

Such the ungentle sport that oft invites
The Spanish maid, and cheers the Spanish swain:
Nurtured in blood betimes, his heart delights
In vengeance, gloating on another's pain.
What private feuds the troubled village stain!
Though now one phalanxed host should meet the foe,
Enough, alas, in humble homes remain,
To meditate 'gainst friends the secret blow,
For some slight cause of wrath, whence life's warm stream must flow.

LXXXI

But Jealousy has fled: his bars, his bolts,
His withered sentinel, duenna sage!
And all whereat the generous soul revolts,
Which the stern dotard deemed he could encage,
Have passed to darkness with the vanished age.
Who late so free as Spanish girls were seen
(Ere War uprose in his volcanic rage),
With braided tresses bounding o'er the green,
While on the gay dance shone Night's lover-loving Queen?

LXXXII

Oh! many a time and oft had Harold loved,
Or dreamed he loved, since rapture is a dream;
But now his wayward bosom was unmoved,
For not yet had he drunk of Lethe's stream:
And lately had he learned with truth to deem
Love has no gift so grateful as his wings:
How fair, how young, how soft soe'er he seem,
Full from the fount of joy's delicious springs
Some bitter o'er the flowers its bubbling venom flings.

LXXXIII

Yet to the beauteous form he was not blind,
Though now it moved him as it moves the wise;
Not that Philosophy on such a mind
E'er deigned to bend her chastely-awful eyes:
But Passion raves itself to rest, or flies;
And Vice, that digs her own voluptuous tomb,
Had buried long his hopes, no more to rise:
Pleasure's palled victim! life-abhorring gloom
Wrote on his faded brow curst Cain's unresting doom.

LXXXIV

Still he beheld, nor mingled with the throng;
But viewed them not with misanthropic hate;
Fain would he now have joined the dance, the song,
But who may smile that sinks beneath his fate?
Nought that he saw his sadness could abate:
Yet once he struggled 'gainst the demon's sway,
And as in Beauty's bower he pensive sate,
Poured forth this unpremeditated lay,
To charms as fair as those that soothed his happier day.

To Inez

Nay, smile not at my sullen brow,
    Alas! I cannot smile again:
Yet Heaven avert that ever thou
    Shouldst weep, and haply weep in vain.

And dost thou ask what secret woe
    I bear, corroding joy and youth?
And wilt thou vainly seek to know
    A pang even thou must fail to soothe?

It is not love, it is not hate,
    Nor low Ambition's honours lost,
That bids me loathe my present state,
    And fly from all I prized the most:

It is that weariness which springs
    From all I meet, or hear, or see:
To me no pleasure Beauty brings;
    Thine eyes have scarce a charm for me.

It is that settled, ceaseless gloom
    The fabled Hebrew wanderer bore,
That will not look beyond the tomb,
    But cannot hope for rest before.

What exile from himself can flee?
    To zones, though more and more remote,
Still, still pursues, where'er I be,
    The blight of life—the demon Thought.

Yet others rapt in pleasure seem,
    And taste of all that I forsake:
Oh! may they still of transport dream,
    And ne'er, at least like me, awake!

Through many a clime 'tis mine to go,
    With many a retrospection curst;
And all my solace is to know,
    Whate'er betides, I've known the worst.

What is that worst? Nay, do not ask—
    In pity from the search forbear:
Smile on—nor venture to unmask
    Man's heart, and view the hell that's there.

LXXXV

Adieu, fair Cadiz! yea, a long adieu!
Who may forget how well thy walls have stood?
When all were changing, thou alone wert true,
First to be free, and last to be subdued.
And if amidst a scene, a shock so rude,
Some native blood was seen thy streets to dye,
A traitor only fell beneath the feud:
Here all were noble, save nobility;
None hugged a conqueror's chain save fallen Chivalry!

LXXXVI

Such be the sons of Spain, and strange her fate!
They fight for freedom, who were never free;
A kingless people for a nerveless state,
Her vassals combat when their chieftains flee,

True to the veriest slaves of Treachery;
Fond of a land which gave them nought but life,
Pride points the path that leads to liberty;
Back to the struggle, baffled in the strife,
War, war is still the cry, 'War even to the knife!'

LXXXVII

Ye, who would more of Spain and Spaniards know,
Go, read whate'er is writ of bloodiest strife:
Whate'er keen Vengeance urged on foreign foe
Can act, is acting there against man's life:
From flashing scimitar to secret knife,
War mouldeth there each weapon to his need—
So may he guard the sister and the wife,
So may he make each curst oppressor bleed,
So may such foes deserve the most remorseless deed!

LXXXVIII

Flows there a tear of pity for the dead?
Look o'er the ravage of the reeking plain:
Look on the hands with female slaughter red;
Then to the dogs resign the unburied slain,
Then to the vulture let each corse remain;
Albeit unworthy of the prey-bird's maw,
Let their bleached bones, and blood's unbleaching stain,
Long mark the battle-field with hideous awe:
Thus only may our sons conceive the scenes we saw!

LXXXIX

Nor yet, alas, the dreadful work is done;
Fresh legions pour adown the Pyrenees:
It deepens still, the work is scarce begun,
Nor mortal eye the distant end foresees.
Fall'n nations gaze on Spain: if freed, she frees
More than her fell Pizarros once enchained.

Strange retribution! now Columbia's ease
Repairs the wrongs that Quito's sons sustained,
While o'er the parent clime prowls Murder unrestrained.

XC

Not all the blood at Talavera shed,
Not all the marvels of Barossa's fight,
Not Albuera lavish of the dead,
Have won for Spain her well-asserted right.
When shall her Olive-Branch be free from blight?
When shall she breathe her from the blushing toil?
How many a doubtful day shall sink in night,
Ere the Frank robber turn him from his spoil,
And Freedom's stranger-tree grow native of the soil?

XCI

And thou, my friend! since unavailing woe
Bursts from my heart, and mingles with the strain—
Had the sword laid thee with the mighty low,
Pride might forbid e'en Friendship to complain:
But thus unlaurelled to descend in vain,
By all forgotten, save the lonely breast,
And mix unbleeding with the boasted slain,
While glory crowns so many a meaner crest!
What hadst thou done, to sink so peacefully to rest?

XCII

Oh, known the earliest, and esteemed the most!
Dear to a heart where nought was left so dear!
Though to my hopeless days for ever lost,
In dreams deny me not to see thee here!
And Morn in secret shall renew the tear
Of Consciousness awaking to her woes,
And Fancy hover o'er thy bloodless bier,
Till my frail frame return to whence it rose,
And mourned and mourner lie united in repose.

XCIII

Here is one fytte of Harold's pilgrimage.
Ye who of him may further seek to know,
Shall find some tidings in a future page,
If he that rhymeth now may scribble moe.
Is this too much? Stern critic, say not so:
Patience! and ye shall hear what he beheld
In other lands, where he was doomed to go:
Lands that contain the monuments of eld,
Ere Greece and Grecian arts by barbarous hands were quelled.

Canto the Second

I

Come, blue-eyed maid of heaven!—but thou, alas,
Didst never yet one mortal song inspire—
Goddess of Wisdom! here thy temple was,
And is, despite of war and wasting fire,
And years, that bade thy worship to expire:
But worse than steel, and flame, and ages slow,
Is the drear sceptre and dominion dire
Of men who never felt the sacred glow
That thoughts of thee and thine on polished breasts bestow.

II

Ancient of days! august Athena! where,
Where are thy men of might, thy grand in soul?
Gone—glimmering through the dream of things that were:
First in the race that led to Glory's goal,
They won, and passed away—is this the whole?
A schoolboy's tale, the wonder of an hour!
The warrior's weapon and the sophist's stole
Are sought in vain, and o'er each mouldering tower,
Dim with the mist of years, grey flits the shade of power.

III

Son of the morning, rise! approach you here!
Come—but molest not yon defenceless urn!
Look on this spot—a nation's sepulchre!
Abode of gods, whose shrines no longer burn.
E'en gods must yield—religions take their turn:
'Twas Jove's—'tis Mahomet's; and other creeds
Will rise with other years, till man shall learn
Vainly his incense soars, his victim bleeds;
Poor child of Doubt and Death, whose hope is built on reeds.

IV

Bound to the earth, he lifts his eyes to heaven—
Is't not enough, unhappy thing, to know
Thou art? Is this a boon so kindly given,
That being, thou wouldst be again, and go,
Thou know'st not, reck'st not to what region, so
On earth no more, but mingled with the skies!
Still wilt thou dream on future joy and woe?
Regard and weigh yon dust before it flies:
That little urn saith more than thousand homilies.

V

Or burst the vanished hero's lofty mound;
Far on the solitary shore he sleeps;
He fell, and falling nations mourned around;
But now not one of saddening thousands weeps,
Nor warlike worshipper his vigil keeps
Where demi-gods appeared, as records tell.
Remove yon skull from out the scattered heaps:
Is that a temple where a God may dwell?
Why, e'en the worm at last disdains her shattered cell!

VI

Look on its broken arch, its ruined wall,
Its chambers desolate, and portals foul:
Yes, this was once Ambition's airy hall,
The dome of Thought, the Palace of the Soul.
Behold through each lack-lustre, eyeless hole,
The gay recess of Wisdom and of Wit,
And Passion's host, that never brooked control:
Can all saint, sage, or sophist ever writ,
People this lonely tower, this tenement refit?

VII

Well didst thou speak, Athena's wisest son!
'All that we know is, nothing can be known.'
Why should we shrink from what we cannot shun?
Each hath its pang, but feeble sufferers groan
With brain-born dreams of evil all their own.
Pursue what chance or fate proclaimeth best;
Peace waits us on the shores of Acheron:
There no forced banquet claims the sated guest,
But Silence spreads the couch of ever welcome rest.

VIII

Yet if, as holiest men have deemed, there be
A land of souls beyond that sable shore,
To shame the doctrine of the Sadducee
And sophists, madly vain of dubious lore;
How sweet it were in concert to adore
With those who made our mortal labours light!
To hear each voice we feared to hear no more!
Behold each mighty shade revealed to sight,
The Bactrian, Samian sage, and all who taught the right!

IX

There, thou!—whose love and life together fled,
Have left me here to love and live in vain—
Twined with my heart, and can I deem thee dead,
When busy memory flashes on my brain?
Well—I will dream that we may meet again,
And woo the vision to my vacant breast:
If aught of young Remembrance then remain,
Be as it may Futurity's behest,
For me 'twere bliss enough to know thy spirit blest!

X

Here let me sit upon this mossy stone,
The marble column's yet unshaken base!
Here, son of Saturn, was thy favourite throne!
Mightiest of many such! Hence let me trace
The latent grandeur of thy dwelling-place.
It may not be: nor even can Fancy's eye
Restore what time hath laboured to deface.
Yet these proud pillars claim no passing sigh;
Unmoved the Moslem sits, the light Greek carols by.

XI

But who, of all the plunderers of yon fane
On high, where Pallas lingered, loth to flee
The latest relic of her ancient reign—
The last, the worst, dull spoiler, who was he?
Blush, Caledonia! such thy son could be!
England! I joy no child he was of thine:
Thy free-born men should spare what once was free;
Yet they could violate each saddening shrine,
And bear these altars o'er the long reluctant brine.

XII

But most the modern Pict's ignoble boast,
To rive what Goth, and Turk, and Time hath spared:
Cold as the crags upon his native coast,
His mind as barren and his heart as hard,
Is he whose head conceived, whose hand prepared,
Aught to displace Athena's poor remains:
Her sons too weak the sacred shrine to guard,
Yet felt some portion of their mother's pains,
And never knew, till then, the weight of Despot's chains.

XIII

What! shall it e'er be said by British tongue
Albion was happy in Athena's tears?
Though in thy name the slaves her bosom wrung,
Tell not the deed to blushing Europe's ears;
The ocean queen, the free Britannia, bears
The last poor plunder from a bleeding land:
Yes, she, whose generous aid her name endears,
Tore down those remnants with a harpy's hand.
Which envious eld forbore, and tyrants left to stand.

XIV

Where was thine aegis, Pallas, that appalled
Stern Alaric and Havoc on their way?
Where Peleus' son? whom Hell in vain enthralled,
His shade from Hades upon that dread day
Bursting to light in terrible array!
What! could not Pluto spare the chief once more,
To scare a second robber from his prey?
Idly he wandered on the Stygian shore,
Nor now preserved the walls he loved to shield before.

XV

Cold is the heart, fair Greece, that looks on thee,
Nor feels as lovers o'er the dust they loved;
Dull is the eye that will not weep to see
Thy walls defaced, thy mouldering shrines removed
By British hands, which it had best behoved
To guard those relics ne'er to be restored.
Curst be the hour when from their isle they roved,
And once again thy hapless bosom gored,
And snatched thy shrinking gods to northern climes abhorred!

XVI

But where is Harold? shall I then forget
To urge the gloomy wanderer o'er the wave?
Little recked he of all that men regret;
No loved one now in feigned lament could rave;
No friend the parting hand extended gave,
Ere the cold stranger passed to other climes.
Hard is his heart whom charms may not enslave;
But Harold felt not as in other times,
And left without a sigh the land of war and crimes.

XVII

He that has sailed upon the dark blue sea,
Has viewed at times, I ween, a full fair sight;
When the fresh breeze is fair as breeze may be,
The white sails set, the gallant frigate tight,
Masts, spires, and strand retiring to the right,
The glorious main expanding o'er the bow,
The convoy spread like wild swans in their flight,
The dullest sailer wearing bravely now,
So gaily curl the waves before each dashing prow.

XVIII

And oh, the little warlike world within!
The well-reeved guns, the netted canopy,
The hoarse command, the busy humming din,
When, at a word, the tops are manned on high:
Hark to the boatswain's call, the cheering cry,
While through the seaman's hand the tackle glides
Or schoolboy midshipman that, standing by,
Strains his shrill pipe, as good or ill betides,
And well the docile crew that skilful urchin guides.

XIX

White is the glassy deck, without a stain,
Where on the watch the staid lieutenant walks:
Look on that part which sacred doth remain
For the lone chieftain, who majestic stalks,
Silent and feared by all: not oft he talks
With aught beneath him, if he would preserve
That strict restraint, which broken, ever baulks
Conquest and Fame: but Britons rarely swerve
From law, however stern, which tends their strength to nerve.

XX

Blow, swiftly blow, thou keel-compelling gale,
Till the broad sun withdraws his lessening ray;
Then must the pennant-bearer slacken sail,
That lagging barks may make their lazy way.
Ah! grievance sore, and listless dull delay,
To waste on sluggish hulks the sweetest breeze!
What leagues are lost before the dawn of day,
Thus loitering pensive on the willing seas,
The flapping sails hauled down to halt for logs like these!

XXI

The moon is up; by Heaven, a lovely eve!
Long streams of light o'er dancing waves expand!
Now lads on shore may sigh, and maids believe:
Such be our fate when we return to land!
Meantime some rude Arion's restless hand
Wakes the brisk harmony that sailors love:
A circle there of merry listeners stand,
Or to some well-known measure featly move,
Thoughtless, as if on shore they still were free to rove.

XXII

Through Calpe's straits survey the steepy shore;
Europe and Afric, on each other gaze!
Lands of the dark-eyed maid and dusky Moor,
Alike beheld beneath pale Hecate's blaze:
How softly on the Spanish shore she plays,
Disclosing rock, and slope, and forest brown,
Distinct, though darkening with her waning phase:
But Mauritania's giant-shadows frown,
From mountain-cliff to coast descending sombre down.

XXIII

'Tis night, when Meditation bids us feel
We once have loved, though love is at an end:
The heart, lone mourner of its baffled zeal,
Though friendless now, will dream it had a friend.
Who with the weight of years would wish to bend,
When Youth itself survives young Love and Joy?
Alas! when mingling souls forget to blend,
Death hath but little left him to destroy!
Ah, happy years! once more who would not be a boy?

XXIV

Thus bending o'er the vessel's laving side,
To gaze on Dian's wave-reflected sphere,
The soul forgets her schemes of Hope and Pride,
And flies unconscious o'er each backward year.
None are so desolate but something dear,
Dearer than self, possesses or possessed
A thought, and claims the homage of a tear;
A flashing pang! of which the weary breast
Would still, albeit in vain, the heavy heart divest.

XXV

To sit on rocks, to muse o'er flood and fell,
To slowly trace the forest's shady scene,
Where things that own not man's dominion dwell,
And mortal foot hath ne'er or rarely been;
To climb the trackless mountain all unseen,
With the wild flock that never needs a fold;
Alone o'er steeps and foaming falls to lean:
This is not solitude; 'tis but to hold
Converse with Nature's charms, and view her stores unrolled.

XXVI

But midst the crowd, the hum, the shock of men,
To hear, to see, to feel, and to possess,
And roam along, the world's tired denizen,
With none who bless us, none whom we can bless;
Minions of splendour shrinking from distress!
None that, with kindred consciousness endued,
If we were not, would seem to smile the less
Of all that flattered, followed, sought, and sued:
This is to be alone; this, this is solitude!

XXVII

More blest the life of godly eremite,
Such as on lonely Athos may be seen,
Watching at eve upon the giant height,
Which looks o'er waves so blue, skies so serene,
That he who there at such an hour hath been,
Will wistful linger on that hallowed spot;
Then slowly tear him from the witching scene,
Sigh forth one wish that such had been his lot,
Then turn to hate a world he had almost forgot.

LORD BYRON

XXVIII

Pass we the long, unvarying course, the track
Oft trod, that never leaves a trace behind;
Pass we the calm, the gale, the change, the tack,
And each well-known caprice of wave and wind;
Pass we the joys and sorrows sailors find,
Cooped in their winged sea-girt citadel;
The foul, the fair, the contrary, the kind,
As breezes rise and fall, and billows swell,
Till on some jocund morn—lo, land! and all is well.

XXIX

But not in silence pass Calypso's isles,
The sister tenants of the middle deep;
There for the weary still a haven smiles,
Though the fair goddess long has ceased to weep,
And o'er her cliffs a fruitless watch to keep
For him who dared prefer a mortal bride:
Here, too, his boy essayed the dreadful leap
Stern Mentor urged from high to yonder tide;
While thus of both bereft, the nymph-queen doubly sighed.

XXX

Her reign is past, her gentle glories gone:
But trust not this; too easy youth, beware!
A mortal sovereign holds her dangerous throne,
And thou mayst find a new Calypso there.
Sweet Florence! could another ever share
This wayward, loveless heart, it would be thine:
But checked by every tie, I may not dare
To cast a worthless offering at thy shrine,
Nor ask so dear a breast to feel one pang for mine.

XXXI

Thus Harold deemed, as on that lady's eye
He looked, and met its beam without a thought,
Save Admiration glancing harmless by:
Love kept aloof, albeit not far remote,
Who knew his votary often lost and caught,
But knew him as his worshipper no more,
And ne'er again the boy his bosom sought:
Since now he vainly urged him to adore,
Well deemed the little god his ancient sway was o'er.

XXXII

Fair Florence found, in sooth with some amaze,
One who, 'twas said, still sighed to all he saw,
Withstand, unmoved, the lustre of her gaze,
Which others hailed with real or mimic awe,
Their hope, their doom, their punishment, their law:
All that gay Beauty from her bondsmen claims:
And much she marvelled that a youth so raw
Nor felt, nor feigned at least, the oft-told flames,
Which, though sometimes they frown, yet rarely anger dames.

XXXIII

Little knew she that seeming marble heart,
Now masked by silence or withheld by pride,
Was not unskilful in the spoiler's art,
And spread its snares licentious far and wide;
Nor from the base pursuit had turned aside,
As long as aught was worthy to pursue:
But Harold on such arts no more relied;
And had he doted on those eyes so blue,
Yet never would he join the lover's whining crew.

XXXIV

Not much he kens, I ween, of woman's breast,
Who thinks that wanton thing is won by sighs;
What careth she for hearts when once possessed?
Do proper homage to thine idol's eyes,
But not too humbly, or she will despise
Thee and thy suit, though told in moving tropes;
Disguise e'en tenderness, if thou art wise;
Brisk Confidence still best with woman copes;
Pique her and soothe in turn, soon Passion crowns thy hopes.

XXXV

'Tis an old lesson: Time approves it true,
And those who know it best deplore it most;
When all is won that all desire to woo,
The paltry prize is hardly worth the cost:
Youth wasted, minds degraded, honour lost,
These are thy fruits, successful Passion! these!
If, kindly cruel, early hope is crossed,
Still to the last it rankles, a disease,
Not to be cured when Love itself forgets to please.

XXXVI

Away! nor let me loiter in my song,
For we have many a mountain path to tread,
And many a varied shore to sail along,
By pensive Sadness, not by Fiction, led—
Climes, fair withal as ever mortal head
Imagined in its little schemes of thought;
Or e'er in new Utopias were read:
To teach man what he might be, or he ought;
If that corrupted thing could ever such be taught.

XXXVII

Dear Nature is the kindest mother still;
Though always changing, in her aspect mild:
From her bare bosom let me take my fill,
Her never-weaned, though not her favoured child.
Oh! she is fairest in her features wild,
Where nothing polished dares pollute her path:
To me by day or night she ever smiled,
Though I have marked her when none other hath,
And sought her more and more, and loved her best in wrath.

XXXVIII

Land of Albania! where Iskander rose;
Theme of the young, and beacon of the wise,
And he his namesake, whose oft-baffled foes,
Shrunk from his deeds of chivalrous emprise:
Land of Albania! let me bend mine eyes
On thee, thou rugged nurse of savage men!
The cross descends, thy minarets arise,
And the pale crescent sparkles in the glen,
Through many a cypress grove within each city's ken.

XXXIX

Childe Harold sailed, and passed the barren spot
Where sad Penelope o'erlooked the wave;
And onward viewed the mount, not yet forgot,
The lover's refuge, and the Lesbian's grave.
Dark Sappho! could not verse immortal save
That breast imbued with such immortal fire?
Could she not live who life eternal gave?
If life eternal may await the lyre,
That only Heaven to which Earth's children may aspire.

XL

'Twas on a Grecian autumn's gentle eve,
Childe Harold hailed Leucadia's cape afar;
A spot he longed to see, nor cared to leave:
Oft did he mark the scenes of vanished war,
Actium, Lepanto, fatal Trafalgar:
Mark them unmoved, for he would not delight
(Born beneath some remote inglorious star)
In themes of bloody fray, or gallant fight,
But loathed the bravo's trade, and laughed at martial wight.

XLI

But when he saw the evening star above
Leucadia's far-projecting rock of woe,
And hailed the last resort of fruitless love,
He felt, or deemed he felt, no common glow:
And as the stately vessel glided slow
Beneath the shadow of that ancient mount,
He watched the billows' melancholy flow,
And, sunk albeit in thought as he was wont,
More placid seemed his eye, and smooth his pallid front.

XLII

Morn dawns; and with it stern Albania's hills,
Dark Suli's rocks, and Pindus' inland peak,
Robed half in mist, bedewed with snowy rills,
Arrayed in many a dun and purple streak,
Arise; and, as the clouds along them break,
Disclose the dwelling of the mountaineer;
Here roams the wolf, the eagle whets his beak,
Birds, beasts of prey, and wilder men appear,
And gathering storms around convulse the closing year.

XLIII

Now Harold felt himself at length alone,
And bade to Christian tongues a long adieu:
Now he adventured on a shore unknown,
Which all admire, but many dread to view:
His breast was armed 'gainst fate, his wants were few:
Peril he sought not, but ne'er shrank to meet:
The scene was savage, but the scene was new;
This made the ceaseless toil of travel sweet,
Beat back keen winter's blast; and welcomed summer's heat.

XLIV

Here the red cross, for still the cross is here,
Though sadly scoffed at by the circumcised,
Forgets that pride to pampered priesthood dear;
Churchman and votary alike despised.
Foul Superstition! howsoe'er disguised,
Idol, saint, virgin, prophet, crescent, cross,
For whatsoever symbol thou art prized,
Thou sacerdotal gain, but general loss!
Who from true worship's gold can separate thy dross.

XLV

Ambracia's gulf behold, where once was lost
A world for woman, lovely, harmless thing!
In yonder rippling bay, their naval host
Did many a Roman chief and Asian king
To doubtful conflict, certain slaughter, bring
Look where the second Caesar's trophies rose,
Now, like the hands that reared them, withering;
Imperial anarchs, doubling human woes!
God! was thy globe ordained for such to win and lose?

XLVI

From the dark barriers of that rugged clime,
E'en to the centre of Illyria's vales,
Childe Harold passed o'er many a mount sublime,
Through lands scarce noticed in historic tales:
Yet in famed Attica such lovely dales
Are rarely seen; nor can fair Tempe boast
A charm they know not; loved Parnassus fails,
Though classic ground, and consecrated most,
To match some spots that lurk within this lowering coast.

XLVII

He passed bleak Pindus, Acherusia's lake,
And left the primal city of the land,
And onwards did his further journey take
To greet Albania's chief, whose dread command
Is lawless law; for with a bloody hand
He sways a nation, turbulent and bold:
Yet here and there some daring mountain-band
Disdain his power, and from their rocky hold
Hurl their defiance far, nor yield, unless to gold.

XLVIII

Monastic Zitza! from thy shady brow,
Thou small, but favoured spot of holy ground!
Where'er we gaze, around, above, below,
What rainbow tints, what magic charms are found!
Rock, river, forest, mountain all abound,
And bluest skies that harmonise the whole:
Beneath, the distant torrent's rushing sound
Tells where the volumed cataract doth roll
Between those hanging rocks, that shock yet please the soul.

XLIX

Amidst the grove that crowns yon tufted hill,
  Which, were it not for many a mountain nigh
  Rising in lofty ranks, and loftier still,
  Might well itself be deemed of dignity,
  The convent's white walls glisten fair on high;
  Here dwells the caloyer, nor rude is he,
  Nor niggard of his cheer: the passer-by
  Is welcome still; nor heedless will he flee
From hence, if he delight kind Nature's sheen to see.

L

Here in the sultriest season let him rest,
  Fresh is the green beneath those aged trees;
  Here winds of gentlest wing will fan his breast,
  From heaven itself he may inhale the breeze:
  The plain is far beneath—oh! let him seize
  Pure pleasure while he can; the scorching ray
  Here pierceth not, impregnate with disease:
  Then let his length the loitering pilgrim lay,
And gaze, untired, the morn, the noon, the eve away.

LI

Dusky and huge, enlarging on the sight,
  Nature's volcanic amphitheatre,
  Chimera's alps extend from left to right:
  Beneath, a living valley seems to stir;
  Flocks play, trees wave, streams flow, the mountain fir
  Nodding above; behold black Acheron!
  Once consecrated to the sepulchre.
  Pluto! if this be hell I look upon,
Close shamed Elysium's gates, my shade shall seek for none.

LII

No city's towers pollute the lovely view;
Unseen is Yanina, though not remote,
Veiled by the screen of hills: here men are few,
Scanty the hamlet, rare the lonely cot;
But, peering down each precipice, the goat
Browseth: and, pensive o'er his scattered flock,
The little shepherd in his white capote
Doth lean his boyish form along the rock,
Or in his cave awaits the tempest's short-lived shock.

LIII

Oh! where, Dodona, is thine aged grove,
Prophetic fount, and oracle divine?
What valley echoed the response of Jove?
What trace remaineth of the Thunderer's shrine?
All, all forgotten—and shall man repine
That his frail bonds to fleeting life are broke?
Cease, fool! the fate of gods may well be thine:
Wouldst thou survive the marble or the oak,
When nations, tongues, and worlds must sink beneath the stroke?

LIV

Epirus' bounds recede, and mountains fail;
Tired of up-gazing still, the wearied eye
Reposes gladly on as smooth a vale
As ever Spring yclad in grassy dye:
E'en on a plain no humble beauties lie,
Where some bold river breaks the long expanse,
And woods along the banks are waving high,
Whose shadows in the glassy waters dance,
Or with the moonbeam sleep in Midnight's solemn trance.

LV

The sun had sunk behind vast Tomerit,
The Laos wide and fierce came roaring by;
The shades of wonted night were gathering yet,
When, down the steep banks winding wearily
Childe Harold saw, like meteors in the sky,
The glittering minarets of Tepalen,
Whose walls o'erlook the stream; and drawing nigh,
He heard the busy hum of warrior-men
Swelling the breeze that sighed along the lengthening glen.

LVI

He passed the sacred harem's silent tower,
And underneath the wide o'erarching gate
Surveyed the dwelling of this chief of power
Where all around proclaimed his high estate.
Amidst no common pomp the despot sate,
While busy preparation shook the court;
Slaves, eunuchs, soldiers, guests, and santons wait;
Within, a palace, and without a fort,
Here men of every clime appear to make resort.

LVII

Richly caparisoned, a ready row
Of armed horse, and many a warlike store,
Circled the wide-extending court below;
Above, strange groups adorned the corridor;
And ofttimes through the area's echoing door,
Some high-capped Tartar spurred his steed away;
The Turk, the Greek, the Albanian, and the Moor,
Here mingled in their many-hued array,
While the deep war-drum's sound announced the close of day.

LVIII

The wild Albanian kirtled to his knee,
With shawl-girt head and ornamented gun,
And gold-embroidered garments, fair to see:
The crimson-scarfed men of Macedon;
The Delhi with his cap of terror on,
And crooked glaive; the lively, supple Greek;
And swarthy Nubia's mutilated son;
The bearded Turk, that rarely deigns to speak,
Master of all around, too potent to be meek,

LIX

Are mixed conspicuous: some recline in groups,
Scanning the motley scene that varies round;
There some grave Moslem to devotion stoops,
And some that smoke, and some that play are found;
Here the Albanian proudly treads the ground;
Half-whispering there the Greek is heard to prate;
Hark! from the mosque the nightly solemn sound,
The muezzin's call doth shake the minaret,
'There is no god but God!—to prayer—lo! God is great!'

LX

Just at this season Ramazani's fast
Through the long day its penance did maintain.
But when the lingering twilight hour was past,
Revel and feast assumed the rule again:
Now all was bustle, and the menial train
Prepared and spread the plenteous board within;
The vacant gallery now seemed made in vain,
But from the chambers came the mingling din,
As page and slave anon were passing out and in.

LXI

Here woman's voice is never heard: apart
And scarce permitted, guarded, veiled, to move,
She yields to one her person and her heart,
Tamed to her cage, nor feels a wish to rove;
For, not unhappy in her master's love,
And joyful in a mother's gentlest cares,
Blest cares! all other feelings far above!
Herself more sweetly rears the babe she bears,
Who never quits the breast, no meaner passion shares.

LXII

In marble-paved pavilion, where a spring
Of living water from the centre rose,
Whose bubbling did a genial freshness fling,
And soft voluptuous couches breathed repose,
Ali reclined, a man of war and woes:
Yet in his lineaments ye cannot trace,
While Gentleness her milder radiance throws
Along that aged venerable face,
The deeds that lurk beneath, and stain him with disgrace.

LXIII

It is not that yon hoary lengthening beard
Ill suits the passions which belong to youth:
Love conquers age—so Hafiz hath averred,
So sings the Teian, and he sings in sooth—
But crimes that scorn the tender voice of ruth,
Beseeming all men ill, but most the man
In years, have marked him with a tiger's tooth:
Blood follows blood, and through their mortal span,
In bloodier acts conclude those who with blood began.

LXIV

Mid many things most new to ear and eye,
The pilgrim rested here his weary feet,
And gazed around on Moslem luxury,
Till quickly wearied with that spacious seat
Of Wealth and Wantonness, the choice retreat
Of sated Grandeur from the city's noise:
And were it humbler, it in sooth were sweet;
But Peace abhorreth artificial joys,
And Pleasure, leagued with Pomp, the zest of both destroys.

LXV

Fierce are Albania's children, yet they lack
Not virtues, were those virtues more mature.
Where is the foe that ever saw their back?
Who can so well the toil of war endure?
Their native fastnesses not more secure
Than they in doubtful time of troublous need:
Their wrath how deadly! but their friendship sure,
When Gratitude or Valour bids them bleed,
Unshaken rushing on where'er their chief may lead.

LXVI

Childe Harold saw them in their chieftain's tower,
Thronging to war in splendour and success;
And after viewed them, when, within their power,
Himself awhile the victim of distress;
That saddening hour when bad men hotlier press:
But these did shelter him beneath their roof,
When less barbarians would have cheered him less,
And fellow-countrymen have stood aloof—
In aught that tries the heart how few withstand the proof!

LXVII

It chanced that adverse winds once drove his bark
Full on the coast of Suli's shaggy shore,
When all around was desolate and dark;
To land was perilous, to sojourn more;
Yet for awhile the mariners forbore,
Dubious to trust where treachery might lurk:
At length they ventured forth, though doubting sore
That those who loathe alike the Frank and Turk
Might once again renew their ancient butcher-work.

LXVIII

Vain fear! the Suliotes stretched the welcome hand,
Led them o'er rocks and past the dangerous swamp,
Kinder than polished slaves, though not so bland,
And piled the hearth, and wrung their garments damp,
And filled the bowl, and trimmed the cheerful lamp,
And spread their fare: though homely, all they had:
Such conduct bears Philanthropy's rare stamp—
To rest the weary and to soothe the sad,
Doth lesson happier men, and shames at least the bad.

LXIX

It came to pass, that when he did address
Himself to quit at length this mountain land,
Combined marauders half-way barred egress,
And wasted far and near with glaive and brand;
And therefore did he take a trusty band
To traverse Acarnania forest wide,
In war well-seasoned, and with labours tanned,
Till he did greet white Achelous' tide,
And from his farther bank Aetolia's wolds espied.

LXX

Where lone Utraikey forms its circling cove,
And weary waves retire to gleam at rest,
How brown the foliage of the green hill's grove,
Nodding at midnight o'er the calm bay's breast,
As winds come whispering lightly from the west,
Kissing, not ruffling, the blue deep's serene:
Here Harold was received a welcome guest;
Nor did he pass unmoved the gentle scene,
For many a joy could he from night's soft presence glean.

LXXI

On the smooth shore the night-fires brightly blazed,
The feast was done, the red wine circling fast,
And he that unawares had there ygazed
With gaping wonderment had stared aghast;
For ere night's midmost, stillest hour was past,
The native revels of the troop began;
Each palikar his sabre from him cast,
And bounding hand in hand, man linked to man,
Yelling their uncouth dirge, long danced the kirtled clan.

LXXII

Childe Harold at a little distance stood,
And viewed, but not displeased, the revelrie,
Nor hated harmless mirth, however rude:
In sooth, it was no vulgar sight to see
Their barbarous, yet their not indecent, glee:
And as the flames along their faces gleamed,
Their gestures nimble, dark eyes flashing free,
The long wild locks that to their girdles streamed,
While thus in concert they this lay half sang, half screamed:

Tambourgi! Tambourgi! thy larum afar
Gives hope to the valiant, and promise of war;
All the sons of the mountains arise at the note,
Chimariot, Illyrian, and dark Suliote!

Oh! who is more brave than a dark Suliote,
To his snowy camese and his shaggy capote?
To the wolf and the vulture he leaves his wild flock,
And descends to the plain like the stream from the rock.

Shall the sons of Chimari, who never forgive
The fault of a friend, bid an enemy live?
Let those guns so unerring such vengeance forego?
What mark is so fair as the breast of a foe?

Macedonia sends forth her invincible race;
For a time they abandon the cave and the chase:
But those scarves of blood-red shall be redder, before
The sabre is sheathed and the battle is o'er.

Then the pirates of Parga that dwell by the waves,
And teach the pale Franks what it is to be slaves,
Shall leave on the beach the long galley and oar,
And track to his covert the captive on shore.

I ask not the pleasure that riches supply,
My sabre shall win what the feeble must buy:
Shall win the young bride with her long flowing hair,
And many a maid from her mother shall tear.

I love the fair face of the maid in her youth;
Her caresses shall lull me, her music shall soothe:
Let her bring from her chamber the many-toned lyre,
And sing us a song on the fall of her sire.

Remember the moment when Previsa fell,
The shrieks of the conquered, the conqueror's yell;
The roofs that we fired, and the plunder we shared,
The wealthy we slaughtered, the lovely we spared.

LORD BYRON

I talk not of mercy, I talk not of fear;
He neither must know who would serve the Vizier;
Since the days of our prophet, the crescent ne'er saw
A chief ever glorious like Ali Pasha.

Dark Muchtar his son to the Danube is sped,
Let the yellow-haired Giaours view his horsetail with dread;
When his Delhis come dashing in blood o'er the banks,
How few shall escape from the Muscovite ranks!

Selictar! unsheath then our chief's scimitar:
Tambourgi! thy larum gives promise of war.
Ye mountains that see us descend to the shore,
Shall view us as victors, or view us no more!

LXXIII

Fair Greece! sad relic of departed worth!
Immortal, though no more; though fallen, great!
Who now shall lead thy scattered children forth,
And long accustomed bondage uncreate?
Not such thy sons who whilome did await,
The hopeless warriors of a willing doom,
In bleak Thermopylae's sepulchral strait—
Oh, who that gallant spirit shall resume,
Leap from Eurotas' banks, and call thee from the tomb?

LXXIV

Spirit of Freedom! when on Phyle's brow
Thou sat'st with Thrasybulus and his train,
Couldst thou forbode the dismal hour which now
Dims the green beauties of thine Attic plain?
Not thirty tyrants now enforce the chain,
But every carle can lord it o'er thy land;
Nor rise thy sons, but idly rail in vain,
Trembling beneath the scourge of Turkish hand,
From birth till death enslaved; in word, in deed, unmanned.

LXXV

In all save form alone, how changed! and who
That marks the fire still sparkling in each eye,
Who would but deem their bosom burned anew
With thy unquenched beam, lost Liberty!
And many dream withal the hour is nigh
That gives them back their fathers' heritage:
For foreign arms and aid they fondly sigh,
Nor solely dare encounter hostile rage,
Or tear their name defiled from Slavery's mournful page.

LXXVI

Hereditary bondsmen! know ye not
Who would be free themselves must strike the blow?
By their right arms the conquest must be wrought?
Will Gaul or Muscovite redress ye? No!
True, they may lay your proud despoilers low,
But not for you will Freedom's altars flame.
Shades of the Helots! triumph o'er your foe:
Greece! change thy lords, thy state is still the same;
Thy glorious day is o'er, but not thy years of shame.

LXXVII

The city won for Allah from the Giaour,
The Giaour from Othman's race again may wrest;
And the Serai's impenetrable tower
Receive the fiery Frank, her former guest;
Or Wahab's rebel brood, who dared divest
The Prophet's tomb of all its pious spoil,
May wind their path of blood along the West;
But ne'er will Freedom seek this fated soil,
But slave succeed to slave through years of endless toil.

LXXVIII

Yet mark their mirth—ere lenten days begin,
That penance which their holy rites prepare
To shrive from man his weight of mortal sin,
By daily abstinence and nightly prayer;
But ere his sackcloth garb Repentance wear,
Some days of joyaunce are decreed to all,
To take of pleasaunce each his secret share,
In motley robe to dance at masking ball,
And join the mimic train of merry Carnival.

LXXIX

And whose more rife with merriment than thine,
O Stamboul! once the empress of their reign?
Though turbans now pollute Sophia's shrine
And Greece her very altars eyes in vain:
(Alas! her woes will still pervade my strain!)
Gay were her minstrels once, for free her throng,
All felt the common joy they now must feign;
Nor oft I've seen such sight, nor heard such song,
As wooed the eye, and thrilled the Bosphorus along.

LXXX

Loud was the lightsome tumult on the shore;
Oft Music changed, but never ceased her tone,
And timely echoed back the measured oar,
And rippling waters made a pleasant moan:
The Queen of tides on high consenting shone;
And when a transient breeze swept o'er the wave,
'Twas as if, darting from her heavenly throne,
A brighter glance her form reflected gave,
Till sparkling billows seemed to light the banks they lave.

LXXXI

Glanced many a light caique along the foam,
Danced on the shore the daughters of the land,
No thought had man or maid of rest or home,
While many a languid eye and thrilling hand
Exchanged the look few bosoms may withstand,
Or gently pressed, returned the pressure still:
Oh Love! young Love! bound in thy rosy band,
Let sage or cynic prattle as he will,
These hours, and only these, redeemed Life's years of ill!

LXXXII

But, midst the throng in merry masquerade,
Lurk there no hearts that throb with secret pain,
E'en through the closest searment half-betrayed?
To such the gentle murmurs of the main
Seem to re-echo all they mourn in vain;
To such the gladness of the gamesome crowd
Is source of wayward thought and stern disdain:
How do they loathe the laughter idly loud,
And long to change the robe of revel for the shroud!

LXXXIII

This must he feel, the true-born son of Greece,
If Greece one true-born patriot can boast:
Not such as prate of war but skulk in peace,
The bondsman's peace, who sighs for all he lost,
Yet with smooth smile his tyrant can accost,
And wield the slavish sickle, not the sword:
Ah, Greece! they love thee least who owe thee most—
Their birth, their blood, and that sublime record
Of hero sires, who shame thy now degenerate horde!

LORD BYRON

LXXXIV

When riseth Lacedaemon's hardihood,
When Thebes Epaminondas rears again,
When Athens' children are with hearts endued,
When Grecian mothers shall give birth to men,
Then mayst thou be restored; but not till then.
A thousand years scarce serve to form a state;
An hour may lay it in the dust: and when
Can man its shattered splendour renovate,
Recall its virtues back, and vanquish Time and Fate?

LXXXV

And yet how lovely in thine age of woe,
Land of lost gods and godlike men, art thou!
Thy vales of evergreen, thy hills of snow,
Proclaim thee Nature's varied favourite now;
Thy fanes, thy temples to the surface bow,
Commingling slowly with heroic earth,
Broke by the share of every rustic plough:
So perish monuments of mortal birth,
So perish all in turn, save well-recorded worth;

LXXXVI

Save where some solitary column mourns
Above its prostrate brethren of the cave;
Save where Tritonia's airy shrine adorns
Colonna's cliff, and gleams along the wave;
Save o'er some warrior's half-forgotten grave,
Where the grey stones and unmolested grass
Ages, but not oblivion, feebly brave,
While strangers only not regardless pass,
Lingering like me, perchance, to gaze, and sigh 'Alas!'

LXXXVII

Yet are thy skies as blue, thy crags as wild:
Sweet are thy groves, and verdant are thy fields,
Thine olives ripe as when Minerva smiled,
And still his honeyed wealth Hymettus yields;
There the blithe bee his fragrant fortress builds,
The freeborn wanderer of thy mountain air;
Apollo still thy long, long summer gilds,
Still in his beam Mendeli's marbles glare;
Art, Glory, Freedom fail, but Nature still is fair.

LXXXVIII

Where'er we tread, 'tis haunted, holy ground;
No earth of thine is lost in vulgar mould,
But one vast realm of wonder spreads around,
And all the Muse's tales seem truly told,
Till the sense aches with gazing to behold
The scenes our earliest dreams have dwelt upon:
Each hill and dale, each deepening glen and wold,
Defies the power which crushed thy temples gone:
Age shakes Athena's tower, but spares gray Marathon.

LXXXIX

The sun, the soil, but not the slave, the same;
Unchanged in all except its foreign lord—
Preserves alike its bounds and boundless fame;
The battle-field, where Persia's victim horde
First bowed beneath the brunt of Hellas' sword,
As on the morn to distant Glory dear,
When Marathon became a magic word;
Which uttered, to the hearer's eye appear
The camp, the host, the fight, the conqueror's career.

XC

The flying Mede, his shaftless broken bow;
The fiery Greek, his red pursuing spear;
Mountains above, Earth's, Ocean's plain below;
Death in the front, Destruction in the rear!
Such was the scene—what now remaineth here?
What sacred trophy marks the hallowed ground,
Recording Freedom's smile and Asia's tear?
The rifled urn, the violated mound,
The dust thy courser's hoof, rude stranger! spurns around.

XCI

Yet to the remnants of thy splendour past
Shall pilgrims, pensive, but unwearied, throng:
Long shall the voyager, with th' Ionian blast,
Hail the bright clime of battle and of song;
Long shall thine annals and immortal tongue
Fill with thy fame the youth of many a shore:
Boast of the aged! lesson of the young!
Which sages venerate and bards adore,
As Pallas and the Muse unveil their awful lore.

XCII

The parted bosom clings to wonted home,
If aught that's kindred cheer the welcome hearth;
He that is lonely, hither let him roam,
And gaze complacent on congenial earth.
Greece is no lightsome land of social mirth;
But he whom Sadness sootheth may abide,
And scarce regret the region of his birth,
When wandering slow by Delphi's sacred side,
Or gazing o'er the plains where Greek and Persian died.

XCIII

Let such approach this consecrated land,
And pass in peace along the magic waste:
But spare its relics—let no busy hand
Deface the scenes, already how defaced!
Not for such purpose were these altars placed.
Revere the remnants nations once revered;
So may our country's name be undisgraced,
So mayst thou prosper where thy youth was reared,
By every honest joy of love and life endeared!

XCIV

For thee, who thus in too protracted song
Hath soothed thine idlesse with inglorious lays,
Soon shall thy voice be lost amid the throng
Of louder minstrels in these later days:
To such resign the strife for fading bays—
Ill may such contest now the spirit move
Which heeds nor keen reproach nor partial praise,
Since cold each kinder heart that might approve,
And none are left to please where none are left to love.

XCV

Thou too art gone, thou loved and lovely one!
Whom youth and youth's affections bound to me;
Who did for me what none beside have done,
Nor shrank from one albeit unworthy thee.
What is my being? thou hast ceased to be!
Nor stayed to welcome here thy wanderer home,
Who mourns o'er hours which we no more shall see—
Would they had never been, or were to come!
Would he had ne'er returned to find fresh cause to roam!

XCVI

Oh! ever loving, lovely, and beloved!
How selfish Sorrow ponders on the past,
And clings to thoughts now better far removed!
But Time shall tear thy shadow from me last.
All thou couldst have of mine, stern Death, thou hast:
The parent, friend, and now the more than friend;
Ne'er yet for one thine arrows flew so fast,
And grief with grief continuing still to blend,
Hath snatched the little joy that life had yet to lend.

XCVII

Then must I plunge again into the crowd,
And follow all that Peace disdains to seek?
Where Revel calls, and Laughter, vainly loud,
False to the heart, distorts the hollow cheek,
To leave the flagging spirit doubly weak!
Still o'er the features, which perforce they cheer,
To feign the pleasure or conceal the pique;
Smiles form the channel of a future tear,
Or raise the writhing lip with ill-dissembled sneer.

XCVIII

What is the worst of woes that wait on age?
What stamps the wrinkle deeper on the brow?
To view each loved one blotted from life's page,
And be alone on earth, as I am now.
Before the Chastener humbly let me bow,
O'er hearts divided and o'er hopes destroyed:
Roll on, vain days! full reckless may ye flow,
Since Time hath reft whate'er my soul enjoyed,
And with the ills of eld mine earlier years alloyed.

Canto the Third

I

Is thy face like thy mother's, my fair child!
Ada! sole daughter of my house and heart?
When last I saw thy young blue eyes, they smiled,
And then we parted,—not as now we part,
But with a hope.—
    Awaking with a start,
The waters heave around me; and on high
The winds lift up their voices: I depart,
Whither I know not; but the hour's gone by,
When Albion's lessening shores could grieve or glad mine eye.

II

Once more upon the waters! yet once more!
And the waves bound beneath me as a steed
That knows his rider. Welcome to their roar!
Swift be their guidance, wheresoe'er it lead!
Though the strained mast should quiver as a reed,
And the rent canvas fluttering strew the gale,
Still must I on; for I am as a weed,
Flung from the rock, on Ocean's foam, to sail
Where'er the surge may sweep, the tempest's breath prevail.

III

In my youth's summer I did sing of One,
The wandering outlaw of his own dark mind;
Again I seize the theme, then but begun,
And bear it with me, as the rushing wind
Bears the cloud onwards: in that tale I find
The furrows of long thought, and dried-up tears,
Which, ebbing, leave a sterile track behind,
O'er which all heavily the journeying years
Plod the last sands of life—where not a flower appears.

IV

Since my young days of passion—joy, or pain,
Perchance my heart and harp have lost a string,
And both may jar: it may be, that in vain
I would essay as I have sung to sing.
Yet, though a dreary strain, to this I cling,
So that it wean me from the weary dream
Of selfish grief or gladness—so it fling
Forgetfulness around me—it shall seem
To me, though to none else, a not ungrateful theme.

V

He who, grown aged in this world of woe,
In deeds, not years, piercing the depths of life,
So that no wonder waits him; nor below
Can love or sorrow, fame, ambition, strife,
Cut to his heart again with the keen knife
Of silent, sharp endurance: he can tell
Why thought seeks refuge in lone caves, yet rife
With airy images, and shapes which dwell
Still unimpaired, though old, in the soul's haunted cell.

VI

'Tis to create, and in creating live
A being more intense, that we endow
With form our fancy, gaining as we give
The life we image, even as I do now.
What am I? Nothing: but not so art thou,
Soul of my thought! with whom I traverse earth,
Invisible but gazing, as I glow
Mixed with thy spirit, blended with thy birth,
And feeling still with thee in my crushed feelings' dearth.

VII

Yet must I think less wildly: I HAVE thought
Too long and darkly, till my brain became,
In its own eddy boiling and o'erwrought,
A whirling gulf of phantasy and flame:
And thus, untaught in youth my heart to tame,
My springs of life were poisoned. 'Tis too late!
Yet am I changed; though still enough the same
In strength to bear what time cannot abate,
And feed on bitter fruits without accusing fate.

VIII

Something too much of this: but now 'tis past,
And the spell closes with its silent seal.
Long-absent Harold reappears at last;
He of the breast which fain no more would feel,
Wrung with the wounds which kill not, but ne'er heal;
Yet Time, who changes all, had altered him
In soul and aspect as in age: years steal
Fire from the mind as vigour from the limb;
And life's enchanted cup but sparkles near the brim.

IX

His had been quaffed too quickly, and he found
The dregs were wormwood; but he filled again,
And from a purer fount, on holier ground,
And deemed its spring perpetual; but in vain!
Still round him clung invisibly a chain
Which galled for ever, fettering though unseen,
And heavy though it clanked not; worn with pain,
Which pined although it spoke not, and grew keen,
Entering with every step he took through many a scene.

X

Secure in guarded coldness, he had mixed
Again in fancied safety with his kind,
And deemed his spirit now so firmly fixed
And sheathed with an invulnerable mind,
That, if no joy, no sorrow lurked behind;
And he, as one, might midst the many stand
Unheeded, searching through the crowd to find
Fit speculation; such as in strange land
He found in wonder-works of God and Nature's hand.

XI

But who can view the ripened rose, nor seek
To wear it? who can curiously behold
The smoothness and the sheen of beauty's cheek,
Nor feel the heart can never all grow old?
Who can contemplate fame through clouds unfold
The star which rises o'er her steep, nor climb?
Harold, once more within the vortex rolled
On with the giddy circle, chasing Time,
Yet with a nobler aim than in his youth's fond prime.

XII

But soon he knew himself the most unfit
Of men to herd with Man; with whom he held
Little in common; untaught to submit
His thoughts to others, though his soul was quelled,
In youth by his own thoughts; still uncompelled,
He would not yield dominion of his mind
To spirits against whom his own rebelled;
Proud though in desolation; which could find
A life within itself, to breathe without mankind.

XIII

Where rose the mountains, there to him were friends;
Where rolled the ocean, thereon was his home;
Where a blue sky, and glowing clime, extends,
He had the passion and the power to roam;
The desert, forest, cavern, breaker's foam,
Were unto him companionship; they spake
A mutual language, clearer than the tome
Of his land's tongue, which he would oft forsake
For nature's pages glassed by sunbeams on the lake.

XIV

Like the Chaldean, he could watch the stars,
Till he had peopled them with beings bright
As their own beams; and earth, and earth-born jars,
And human frailties, were forgotten quite:
Could he have kept his spirit to that flight,
He had been happy; but this clay will sink
Its spark immortal, envying it the light
To which it mounts, as if to break the link
That keeps us from yon heaven which woos us to its brink.

XV

But in Man's dwellings he became a thing
Restless and worn, and stern and wearisome,
Drooped as a wild-born falcon with clipt wing,
To whom the boundless air alone were home:
Then came his fit again, which to o'ercome,
As eagerly the barred-up bird will beat
His breast and beak against his wiry dome
Till the blood tinge his plumage, so the heat
Of his impeded soul would through his bosom eat.

XVI

Self-exiled Harold wanders forth again,
With naught of hope left, but with less of gloom;
The very knowledge that he lived in vain,
That all was over on this side the tomb,
Had made Despair a smilingness assume,
Which, though 'twere wild—as on the plundered wreck
When mariners would madly meet their doom
With draughts intemperate on the sinking deck—
Did yet inspire a cheer, which he forbore to check.

XVII

Stop! for thy tread is on an empire's dust!
An earthquake's spoil is sepulchred below!
Is the spot marked with no colossal bust?
Nor column trophied for triumphal show?
None; but the moral's truth tells simpler so,
As the ground was before, thus let it be;—
How that red rain hath made the harvest grow!
And is this all the world has gained by thee,
Thou first and last of fields! king-making Victory?

XVIII

And Harold stands upon this place of skulls,
The grave of France, the deadly Waterloo!
How in an hour the power which gave annuls
Its gifts, transferring fame as fleeting too!
In 'pride of place' here last the eagle flew,
Then tore with bloody talon the rent plain,
Pierced by the shaft of banded nations through:
Ambition's life and labours all were vain;
He wears the shattered links of the world's broken chain.

XIX

Fit retribution! Gaul may champ the bit,
And foam in fetters, but is Earth more free?
Did nations combat to make ONE submit;
Or league to teach all kings true sovereignty?
What! shall reviving thraldom again be
The patched-up idol of enlightened days?
Shall we, who struck the Lion down, shall we
Pay the Wolf homage? proffering lowly gaze
And servile knees to thrones? No; PROVE before ye praise!

XX

If not, o'er one fall'n despot boast no more!
In vain fair cheeks were furrowed with hot tears
For Europe's flowers long rooted up before
The trampler of her vineyards; in vain years
Of death, depopulation, bondage, fears,
Have all been borne, and broken by the accord
Of roused-up millions: all that most endears
Glory, is when the myrtle wreathes a sword
Such as Harmodius drew on Athens' tyrant lord.

XXI

There was a sound of revelry by night,
And Belgium's capital had gathered then
Her Beauty and her Chivalry, and bright
The lamps shone o'er fair women and brave men;
A thousand hearts beat happily; and when
Music arose with its voluptuous swell,
Soft eyes looked love to eyes which spake again,
And all went merry as a marriage bell;
But hush! hark! a deep sound strikes like a rising knell!

XXII

Did ye not hear it?—No; 'twas but the wind,
Or the car rattling o'er the stony street;
On with the dance! let joy be unconfined;
No sleep till morn, when Youth and Pleasure meet
To chase the glowing Hours with flying feet.
But hark!—that heavy sound breaks in once more,
As if the clouds its echo would repeat;
And nearer, clearer, deadlier than before!
Arm! arm! it is—it is—the cannon's opening roar!

XXIII

Within a windowed niche of that high hall
Sate Brunswick's fated chieftain; he did hear
That sound, the first amidst the festival,
And caught its tone with Death's prophetic ear;
And when they smiled because he deemed it near,
His heart more truly knew that peal too well
Which stretched his father on a bloody bier,
And roused the vengeance blood alone could quell:
He rushed into the field, and, foremost fighting, fell.

XXIV

Ah! then and there was hurrying to and fro,
And gathering tears, and tremblings of distress,
And cheeks all pale, which but an hour ago
Blushed at the praise of their own loveliness;
And there were sudden partings, such as press
The life from out young hearts, and choking sighs
Which ne'er might be repeated: who would guess
If ever more should meet those mutual eyes,
Since upon night so sweet such awful morn could rise!

XXV

And there was mounting in hot haste: the steed,
The mustering squadron, and the clattering car,
Went pouring forward with impetuous speed,
And swiftly forming in the ranks of war;
And the deep thunder peal on peal afar;
And near, the beat of the alarming drum
Roused up the soldier ere the morning star;
While thronged the citizens with terror dumb,
Or whispering, with white lips—'The foe! They come! they come!'

XXVI

And wild and high the 'Cameron's gathering' rose,
The war-note of Lochiel, which Albyn's hills
Have heard, and heard, too, have her Saxon foes:
How in the noon of night that pibroch thrills
Savage and shrill! But with the breath which fills
Their mountain-pipe, so fill the mountaineers
With the fierce native daring which instils
The stirring memory of a thousand years,
And Evan's, Donald's fame rings in each clansman's ears.

XXVII

And Ardennes waves above them her green leaves,
Dewy with Nature's tear-drops, as they pass,
Grieving, if aught inanimate e'er grieves,
Over the unreturniug brave,—alas!
Ere evening to be trodden like the grass
Which now beneath them, but above shall grow
In its next verdure, when this fiery mass
Of living valour, rolling on the foe,
And burning with high hope, shall moulder cold and low.

XXVIII

Last noon beheld them full of lusty life,
Last eve in Beauty's circle proudly gay,
The midnight brought the signal-sound of strife,
The morn the marshalling in arms,—the day
Battle's magnificently stern array!
The thunder-clouds close o'er it, which when rent
The earth is covered thick with other clay,
Which her own clay shall cover, heaped and pent,
Rider and horse,—friend, foe,—in one red burial blent!

XXIX

Their praise is hymned by loftier harps than mine;
Yet one I would select from that proud throng,
Partly because they blend me with his line,
And partly that I did his sire some wrong,
And partly that bright names will hallow song;
And his was of the bravest, and when showered
The death-bolts deadliest the thinned files along,
Even where the thickest of war's tempest lowered,
They reached no nobler breast than thine, young, gallant Howard!

XXX

There have been tears and breaking hearts for thee,
And mine were nothing, had I such to give;
But when I stood beneath the fresh green tree,
Which living waves where thou didst cease to live,
And saw around me the wild field revive
With fruits and fertile promise, and the Spring
Come forth her work of gladness to contrive,
With all her reckless birds upon the wing,
I turned from all she brought to those she could not bring.

XXXI

I turned to thee, to thousands, of whom each
And one as all a ghastly gap did make
In his own kind and kindred, whom to teach
Forgetfulness were mercy for their sake;
The Archangel's trump, not Glory's, must awake
Those whom they thirst for; though the sound of Fame
May for a moment soothe, it cannot slake
The fever of vain longing, and the name
So honoured, but assumes a stronger, bitterer claim.

XXXII

They mourn, but smile at length; and, smiling, mourn:
The tree will wither long before it fall:
The hull drives on, though mast and sail be torn;
The roof-tree sinks, but moulders on the hall
In massy hoariness; the ruined wall
Stands when its wind-worn battlements are gone;
The bars survive the captive they enthral;
The day drags through though storms keep out the sun;
And thus the heart will break, yet brokenly live on:

XXXIII

E'en as a broken mirror, which the glass
In every fragment multiplies; and makes
A thousand images of one that was,
The same, and still the more, the more it breaks;
And thus the heart will do which not forsakes,
Living in shattered guise, and still, and cold,
And bloodless, with its sleepless sorrow aches,
Yet withers on till all without is old,
Showing no visible sign, for such things are untold.

XXXIV

There is a very life in our despair,
Vitality of poison,—a quick root
Which feeds these deadly branches; for it were
As nothing did we die; but life will suit
Itself to Sorrow's most detested fruit,
Like to the apples on the Dead Sea shore,
All ashes to the taste: Did man compute
Existence by enjoyment, and count o'er
Such hours 'gainst years of life,—say, would he name threescore?

XXXV

The Psalmist numbered out the years of man:
They are enough: and if thy tale be TRUE,
Thou, who didst grudge him e'en that fleeting span,
More than enough, thou fatal Waterloo!
Millions of tongues record thee, and anew
Their children's lips shall echo them, and say,
'Here, where the sword united nations drew,
Our countrymen were warring on that day!'
And this is much, and all which will not pass away.

XXXVI

There sunk the greatest, nor the worst of men,
Whose spirit anithetically mixed
One moment of the mightiest, and again
On little objects with like firmness fixed;
Extreme in all things! hadst thou been betwixt,
Thy throne had still been thine, or never been;
For daring made thy rise as fall: thou seek'st
Even now to reassume the imperial mien,
And shake again the world, the Thunderer of the scene!

XXXVII

Conqueror and captive of the earth art thou!
She trembles at thee still, and thy wild name
Was ne'er more bruited in men's minds than now
That thou art nothing, save the jest of Fame,
Who wooed thee once, thy vassal, and became
The flatterer of thy fierceness, till thou wert
A god unto thyself; nor less the same
To the astounded kingdoms all inert,
Who deemed thee for a time whate'er thou didst assert.

XXXVIII

Oh, more or less than man—in high or low,
Battling with nations, flying from the field;
Now making monarchs' necks thy footstool, now
More than thy meanest soldier taught to yield:
An empire thou couldst crush, command, rebuild,
But govern not thy pettiest passion, nor,
However deeply in men's spirits skilled,
Look through thine own, nor curb the lust of war,
Nor learn that tempted Fate will leave the loftiest star.

XXXIX

Yet well thy soul hath brooked the turning tide
With that untaught innate philosophy,
Which, be it wisdom, coldness, or deep pride,
Is gall and wormwood to an enemy.
When the whole host of hatred stood hard by,
To watch and mock thee shrinking, thou hast smiled
With a sedate and all-enduring eye;
When Fortune fled her spoiled and favourite child,
He stood unbowed beneath the ills upon him piled.

XL

Sager than in thy fortunes; for in them
Ambition steeled thee on to far too show
That just habitual scorn, which could contemn
Men and their thoughts; 'twas wise to feel, not so
To wear it ever on thy lip and brow,
And spurn the instruments thou wert to use
Till they were turned unto thine overthrow:
'Tis but a worthless world to win or lose;
So hath it proved to thee, and all such lot who choose.

XLI

If, like a tower upon a headland rock,
Thou hadst been made to stand or fall alone,
Such scorn of man had helped to brave the shock;
But men's thoughts were the steps which paved thy throne,
Their admiration thy best weapon shone;
The part of Philip's son was thine, not then
(Unless aside thy purple had been thrown)
Like stern Diogenes to mock at men;
For sceptred cynics earth were far too wide a den.

XLII

But quiet to quick bosoms is a hell,
And There hath been thy bane; there is a fire
And motion of the soul, which will not dwell
In its own narrow being, but aspire
Beyond the fitting medium of desire;
And, but once kindled, quenchless evermore,
Preys upon high adventure, nor can tire
Of aught but rest; a fever at the core,
Fatal to him who bears, to all who ever bore.

XLIII

This makes the madmen who have made men mad
By their contagion! Conquerors and Kings,
Founders of sects and systems, to whom add
Sophists, Bards, Statesmen, all unquiet things
Which stir too strongly the soul's secret springs,
And are themselves the fools to those they fool;
Envied, yet how unenviable! what stings
Are theirs! One breast laid open were a school
Which would unteach mankind the lust to shine or rule:

XLIV

Their breath is agitation, and their life
A storm whereon they ride, to sink at last,
And yet so nursed and bigoted to strife,
That should their days, surviving perils past,
Melt to calm twilight, they feel overcast
With sorrow and supineness, and so die;
Even as a flame unfed, which runs to waste
With its own flickering, or a sword laid by,
Which eats into itself, and rusts ingloriously.

XLV

He who ascends to mountain-tops, shall find
The loftiest peaks most wrapt in clouds and snow;
He who surpasses or subdues mankind,
Must look down on the hate of those below.
Though high ABOVE the sun of glory glow,
And far BENEATH the earth and ocean spread,
ROUND him are icy rocks, and loudly blow
Contending tempests on his naked head,
And thus reward the toils which to those summits led.

XLVI

Away with these; true Wisdom's world will be
Within its own creation, or in thine,
Maternal Nature! for who teems like thee,
Thus on the banks of thy majestic Rhine?
There Harold gazes on a work divine,
A blending of all beauties; streams and dells,
Fruit, foliage, crag, wood, corn-field, mountain, vine,
And chiefless castles breathing stern farewells
From grey but leafy walls, where Ruin greenly dwells.

XLVII

And there they stand, as stands a lofty mind,
Worn, but unstooping to the baser crowd,
All tenantless, save to the crannying wind,
Or holding dark communion with the cloud.
There was a day when they were young and proud,
Banners on high, and battles passed below;
But they who fought are in a bloody shroud,
And those which waved are shredless dust ere now,
And the bleak battlements shall bear no future blow.

XLVIII

Beneath these battlements, within those walls,
Power dwelt amidst her passions; in proud state
Each robber chief upheld his armed halls,
Doing his evil will, nor less elate
Than mightier heroes of a longer date.
What want these outlaws conquerors should have
But History's purchased page to call them great?
A wider space, an ornamented grave?
Their hopes were not less warm, their souls were full as brave.

XLIX

In their baronial feuds and single fields,
What deeds of prowess unrecorded died!
And Love, which lent a blazon to their shields,
With emblems well devised by amorous pride,
Through all the mail of iron hearts would glide;
But still their flame was fierceness, and drew on
Keen contest and destruction near allied,
And many a tower for some fair mischief won,
Saw the discoloured Rhine beneath its ruin run.

L

But thou, exulting and abounding river!
Making thy waves a blessing as they flow
Through banks whose beauty would endure for ever,
Could man but leave thy bright creation so,
Nor its fair promise from the surface mow
With the sharp scythe of conflict,—then to see
Thy valley of sweet waters, were to know
Earth paved like Heaven; and to seem such to me
Even now what wants thy stream?—that it should Lethe be.

LI

A thousand battles have assailed thy banks,
But these and half their fame have passed away,
And Slaughter heaped on high his weltering ranks:
Their very graves are gone, and what are they?
Thy tide washed down the blood of yesterday,
And all was stainless, and on thy clear stream
Glassed with its dancing light the sunny ray;
But o'er the blackened memory's blighting dream
Thy waves would vainly roll, all sweeping as they seem.

　　　　　　　　　　　　　　　　　　　　　　　　　　　LORD BYRON

LII

Thus Harold inly said, and passed along,
Yet not insensible to all which here
Awoke the jocund birds to early song
In glens which might have made e'en exile dear:
Though on his brow were graven lines austere,
And tranquil sternness which had ta'en the place
Of feelings fierier far but less severe,
Joy was not always absent from his face,
But o'er it in such scenes would steal with transient trace.

LIII

Nor was all love shut from him, though his days
Of passion had consumed themselves to dust.
It is in vain that we would coldly gaze
On such as smile upon us; the heart must
Leap kindly back to kindness, though disgust
Hath weaned it from all worldlings: thus he felt,
For there was soft remembrance, and sweet trust
In one fond breast, to which his own would melt,
And in its tenderer hour on that his bosom dwelt.

LIV

And he had learned to love,—I know not why,
For this in such as him seems strange of mood,—
The helpless looks of blooming infancy,
Even in its earliest nurture; what subdued,
To change like this, a mind so far imbued
With scorn of man, it little boots to know;
But thus it was; and though in solitude
Small power the nipped affections have to grow,
In him this glowed when all beside had ceased to glow.

LV

And there was one soft breast, as hath been said,
Which unto his was bound by stronger ties
Than the church links withal; and, though unwed,
THAT love was pure, and, far above disguise,
Had stood the test of mortal enmities
Still undivided, and cemented more
By peril, dreaded most in female eyes;
But this was firm, and from a foreign shore
Well to that heart might his these absent greetings pour!

The castled crag of Drachenfels
Frowns o'er the wide and winding Rhine.
Whose breast of waters broadly swells
Between the banks which bear the vine,
And hills all rich with blossomed trees,
And fields which promise corn and wine,
And scattered cities crowning these,
Whose far white walls along them shine,
Have strewed a scene, which I should see
With double joy wert THOU with me!

And peasant girls, with deep blue eyes,
And hands which offer early flowers,
Walk smiling o'er this paradise;
Above, the frequent feudal towers
Through green leaves lift their walls of grey,
And many a rock which steeply lours,
And noble arch in proud decay,
Look o'er this vale of vintage bowers:
But one thing want these banks of Rhine,—
Thy gentle hand to clasp in mine!

I send the lilies given to me;
Though long before thy hand they touch,
I know that they must withered be,
But yet reject them not as such;
For I have cherished them as dear,

Because they yet may meet thine eye,
And guide thy soul to mine e'en here,
When thou behold'st them drooping nigh,
And know'st them gathered by the Rhine,
And offered from my heart to thine!

The river nobly foams and flows,
The charm of this enchanted ground,
And all its thousand turns disclose
Some fresher beauty varying round;
The haughtiest breast its wish might bound
Through life to dwell delighted here;
Nor could on earth a spot be found
To Nature and to me so dear,
Could thy dear eyes in following mine
Still sweeten more these banks of Rhine!

LVI

By Coblentz, on a rise of gentle ground,
There is a small and simple pyramid,
Crowning the summit of the verdant mound;
Beneath its base are heroes' ashes hid,
Our enemy's,—but let not that forbid
Honour to Marceau! o'er whose early tomb
Tears, big tears, gushed from the rough soldier's lid,
Lamenting and yet envying such a doom,
Falling for France, whose rights he battled to resume.

LVII

Brief, brave, and glorious was his young career,—
His mourners were two hosts, his friends and foes;
And fitly may the stranger lingering here
Pray for his gallant spirit's bright repose;
For he was Freedom's champion, one of those,
The few in number, who had not o'erstept
The charter to chastise which she bestows

On such as wield her weapons; he had kept
The whiteness of his soul, and thus men o'er him wept.

LVIII

Here Ehrenbreitstein, with her shattered wall
Black with the miner's blast, upon her height
Yet shows of what she was, when shell and ball
Rebounding idly on her strength did light;
A tower of victory! from whence the flight
Of baffled foes was watched along the plain;
But Peace destroyed what War could never blight,
And laid those proud roofs bare to Summer's rain—
On which the iron shower for years had poured in vain.

LIX

Adieu to thee, fair Rhine! How long, delighted,
The stranger fain would linger on his way;
Thine is a scene alike where souls united
Or lonely Contemplation thus might stray;
And could the ceaseless vultures cease to prey
On self-condemning bosoms, it were here,
Where Nature, not too sombre nor too gay,
Wild but not rude, awful yet not austere,
Is to the mellow earth as autumn to the year.

LX

Adieu to thee again! a vain adieu!
There can be no farewell to scene like thine;
The mind is coloured by thy every hue;
And if reluctantly the eyes resign
Their cherished gaze upon thee, lovely Rhine!
'Tis with the thankful glance of parting praise;
More mighty spots may rise—more glaring shine,
But none unite in one attaching maze
The brilliant, fair, and soft;—the glories of old days.

LXI

The negligently grand, the fruitful bloom
Of coming ripeness, the white city's sheen,
The rolling stream, the precipice's gloom,
The forest's growth, and Gothic walls between,
The wild rocks shaped as they had turrets been
In mockery of man's art; and these withal
A race of faces happy as the scene,
Whose fertile bounties here extend to all,
Still springing o'er thy banks, though empires near them fall.

LXII

But these recede. Above me are the Alps,
The palaces of Nature, whose vast walls
Have pinnacled in clouds their snowy scalps,
And throned Eternity in icy halls
Of cold sublimity, where forms and falls
The avalanche—the thunderbolt of snow!
All that expands the spirit, yet appals,
Gathers around these summits, as to show
How Earth may pierce to Heaven, yet leave vain man below.

LXIII

But ere these matchless heights I dare to scan,
There is a spot should not be passed in vain,—
Morat! the proud, the patriot field! where man
May gaze on ghastly trophies of the slain,
Nor blush for those who conquered on that plain;
Here Burgundy bequeathed his tombless host,
A bony heap, through ages to remain,
Themselves their monument;—the Stygian coast
Unsepulchred they roamed, and shrieked each wandering ghost.

LXIV

While Waterloo with Cannae's carnage vies,
Morat and Marathon twin names shall stand;
They were true Glory's stainless victories,
Won by the unambitious heart and hand
Of a proud, brotherly, and civic band,
All unbought champions in no princely cause
Of vice-entailed Corruption; they no land
Doomed to bewail the blasphemy of laws
Making king's rights divine, by some Draconic clause.

LXV

By a lone wall a lonelier column rears
A grey and grief-worn aspect of old days
'Tis the last remnant of the wreck of years,
And looks as with the wild bewildered gaze
Of one to stone converted by amaze,
Yet still with consciousness; and there it stands,
Making a marvel that it not decays,
When the coeval pride of human hands,
Levelled Aventicum, hath strewed her subject lands.

LXVI

And there—oh! sweet and sacred be the name!—
Julia—the daughter, the devoted—gave
Her youth to Heaven; her heart, beneath a claim
Nearest to Heaven's, broke o'er a father's grave.
Justice is sworn 'gainst tears, and hers would crave
The life she lived in; but the judge was just,
And then she died on him she could not save.
Their tomb was simple, and without a bust,
And held within their urn one mind, one heart, one dust.

LXVII

But these are deeds which should not pass away,
And names that must not wither, though the earth
Forgets her empires with a just decay,
The enslavers and the enslaved, their death and birth;
The high, the mountain-majesty of worth,
Should be, and shall, survivor of its woe,
And from its immortality look forth
In the sun's face, like yonder Alpine snow,
Imperishably pure beyond all things below.

LXVIII

Lake Leman woos me with its crystal face,
The mirror where the stars and mountains view
The stillness of their aspect in each trace
Its clear depth yields of their far height and hue:
There is too much of man here, to look through
With a fit mind the might which I behold;
But soon in me shall Loneliness renew
Thoughts hid, but not less cherished than of old,
Ere mingling with the herd had penned me in their fold.

LXIX

To fly from, need not be to hate, mankind;
All are not fit with them to stir and toil,
Nor is it discontent to keep the mind
Deep in its fountain, lest it overboil
In one hot throng, where we become the spoil
Of our infection, till too late and long
We may deplore and struggle with the coil,
In wretched interchange of wrong for wrong
Midst a contentious world, striving where none are strong.

LXX

There, in a moment, we may plunge our years
In fatal penitence, and in the blight
Of our own soul, turn all our blood to tears,
And colour things to come with hues of Night;
The race of life becomes a hopeless flight
To those that walk in darkness: on the sea,
The boldest steer but where their ports invite,
But there are wanderers o'er Eternity
Whose bark drives on and on, and anchored ne'er shall be.

LXXI

Is it not better, then, to be alone,
And love Earth only for its earthly sake?
By the blue rushing of the arrowy Rhone,
Or the pure bosom of its nursing lake,
Which feeds it as a mother who doth make
A fair but froward infant her own care,
Kissing its cries away as these awake;—
Is it not better thus our lives to wear,
Than join the crushing crowd, doomed to inflict or bear?

LXXII

I live not in myself, but I become
Portion of that around me; and to me,
High mountains are a feeling, but the hum
Of human cities torture: I can see
Nothing to loathe in Nature, save to be
A link reluctant in a fleshly chain,
Classed among creatures, when the soul can flee,
And with the sky, the peak, the heaving plain
Of ocean, or the stars, mingle, and not in vain.

LXXIII

And thus I am absorbed, and this is life:
I look upon the peopled desert Past,
As on a place of agony and strife,
Where, for some sin, to Sorrow I was cast,
To act and suffer, but remount at last
With a fresh pinion; which I felt to spring,
Though young, yet waxing vigorous as the blast
Which it would cope with, on delighted wing,
Spurning the clay-cold bonds which round our being cling.

LXXIV

And when, at length, the mind shall be all free
From what it hates in this degraded form,
Reft of its carnal life, save what shall be
Existent happier in the fly and worm,—
When elements to elements conform,
And dust is as it should be, shall I not
Feel all I see, less dazzling, but more warm?
The bodiless thought? the Spirit of each spot?
Of which, even now, I share at times the immortal lot?

LXXV

Are not the mountains, waves, and skies a part
Of me and of my soul, as I of them?
Is not the love of these deep in my heart
With a pure passion? should I not contemn
All objects, if compared with these? and stem
A tide of suffering, rather than forego
Such feelings for the hard and worldly phlegm
Of those whose eyes are only turned below,
Gazing upon the ground, with thoughts which dare not glow?

LXXVI

But this is not my theme; and I return
To that which is immediate, and require
Those who find contemplation in the urn,
To look on One whose dust was once all fire,
A native of the land where I respire
The clear air for awhile—a passing guest,
Where he became a being,—whose desire
Was to be glorious; 'twas a foolish quest,
The which to gain and keep he sacrificed all rest.

LXXVII

Here the self-torturing sophist, wild Rousseau,
The apostle of affliction, he who threw
Enchantment over passion, and from woe
Wrung overwhelming eloquence, first drew
The breath which made him wretched; yet he knew
How to make madness beautiful, and cast
O'er erring deeds and thoughts a heavenly hue
Of words, like sunbeams, dazzling as they past
The eyes, which o'er them shed tears feelingly and fast.

LXXVIII

His love was passion's essence—as a tree
On fire by lightning; with ethereal flame
Kindled he was, and blasted; for to be
Thus, and enamoured, were in him the same.
But his was not the love of living dame,
Nor of the dead who rise upon our dreams,
But of Ideal beauty, which became
In him existence, and o'erflowing teems
Along his burning page, distempered though it seems.

LXXIX

Tнιs breathed itself to life in Julie, Tнιs
Invested her with all that's wild and sweet;
This hallowed, too, the memorable kiss
Which every morn his fevered lip would greet,
From hers, who but with friendship his would meet:
But to that gentle touch, through brain and breast
Flashed the thrilled spirit's love-devouring heat;
In that absorbing sigh perchance more blest,
Than vulgar minds may be with all they seek possest.

LXXX

His life was one long war with self-sought foes,
Or friends by him self-banished; for his mind
Had grown Suspicion's sanctuary, and chose
For its own cruel sacrifice, the kind,
'Gainst whom he raged with fury strange and blind.
But he was frenzied,—wherefore, who may know?
Since cause might be which skill could never find;
But he was frenzied by disease or woe
To that worst pitch of all, which wears a reasoning show.

LXXXI

For then he was inspired, and from him came,
As from the Pythian's mystic cave of yore,
Those oracles which set the world in flame,
Nor ceased to burn till kingdoms were no more:
Did he not this for France, which lay before
Bowed to the inborn tyranny of years?
Broken and trembling to the yoke she bore,
Till by the voice of him and his compeers
Roused up to too much wrath, which follows o'ergrown fears?

LXXXII

They made themselves a fearful monument!
The wreck of old opinions—things which grew,
Breathed from the birth of time: the veil they rent,
And what behind it lay, all earth shall view.
But good with ill they also overthrew,
Leaving but ruins, wherewith to rebuild
Upon the same foundation, and renew
Dungeons and thrones, which the same hour refilled,
As heretofore, because ambition was self-willed.

LXXXIII

But this will not endure, nor be endured!
Mankind have felt their strength, and made it felt.
They might have used it better, but, allured
By their new vigour, sternly have they dealt
On one another; Pity ceased to melt
With her once natural charities. But they,
Who in Oppression's darkness caved had dwelt,
They were not eagles, nourished with the day;
What marvel then, at times, if they mistook their prey?

LXXXIV

What deep wounds ever closed without a scar?
The heart's bleed longest, and but heal to wear
That which disfigures it; and they who war
With their own hopes, and have been vanquished, bear
Silence, but not submission: in his lair
Fixed Passion holds his breath, until the hour
Which shall atone for years; none need despair:
It came, it cometh, and will come,—the power
To punish or forgive—in ONE we shall be slower.

LXXXV

Clear, placid Leman! thy contrasted lake,
With the wild world I dwelt in, is a thing
Which warns me, with its stillness, to forsake
Earth's troubled waters for a purer spring.
This quiet sail is as a noiseless wing
To waft me from distraction; once I loved
Torn ocean's roar, but thy soft murmuring
Sounds sweet as if a sister's voice reproved,
That I with stern delights should e'er have been so moved.

LXXXVI

It is the hush of night, and all between
Thy margin and the mountains, dusk, yet clear,
Mellowed and mingling, yet distinctly seen.
Save darkened Jura, whose capt heights appear
Precipitously steep; and drawing near,
There breathes a living fragrance from the shore,
Of flowers yet fresh with childhood; on the ear
Drops the light drip of the suspended oar,
Or chirps the grasshopper one good-night carol more;

LXXXVII

He is an evening reveller, who makes
His life an infancy, and sings his fill;
At intervals, some bird from out the brakes
Starts into voice a moment, then is still.
There seems a floating whisper on the hill,
But that is fancy, for the starlight dews
All silently their tears of love instil,
Weeping themselves away, till they infuse
Deep into Nature's breast the spirit of her hues.

LXXXVIII

Ye stars! which are the poetry of heaven,
If in your bright leaves we would read the fate
Of men and empires,—'tis to be forgiven,
That in our aspirations to be great,
Our destinies o'erleap their mortal state,
And claim a kindred with you; for ye are
A beauty and a mystery, and create
In us such love and reverence from afar,
That fortune, fame, power, life, have named themselves a star.

LXXXIX

All heaven and earth are still—though not in sleep,
But breathless, as we grow when feeling most;
And silent, as we stand in thoughts too deep:—
All heaven and earth are still: from the high host
Of stars, to the lulled lake and mountain-coast,
All is concentered in a life intense,
Where not a beam, nor air, nor leaf is lost,
But hath a part of being, and a sense
Of that which is of all Creator and defence.

XC

Then stirs the feeling infinite, so felt
In solitude, where we are LEAST alone;
A truth, which through our being then doth melt,
And purifies from self: it is a tone,
The soul and source of music, which makes known
Eternal harmony, and sheds a charm,
Like to the fabled Cytherea's zone,
Binding all things with beauty;—'twould disarm
The spectre Death, had he substantial power to harm.

XCI

Nor vainly did the early Persian make
His altar the high places and the peak
Of earth-o'ergazing mountains, and thus take
A fit and unwalled temple, there to seek
The Spirit, in whose honour shrines are weak,
Upreared of human hands. Come, and compare
Columns and idol-dwellings, Goth or Greek,
With Nature's realms of worship, earth and air,
Nor fix on fond abodes to circumscribe thy prayer!

XCII

The sky is changed!—and such a change! O night,
And storm, and darkness, ye are wondrous strong,
Yet lovely in your strength, as is the light
Of a dark eye in woman! Far along,
From peak to peak, the rattling crags among,
Leaps the live thunder! Not from one lone cloud,
But every mountain now hath found a tongue;
And Jura answers, through her misty shroud,
Back to the joyous Alps, who call to her aloud!

XCIII

And this is in the night:—Most glorious night!
Thou wert not sent for slumber! let me be
A sharer in thy fierce and far delight—
A portion of the tempest and of thee!
How the lit lake shines, a phosphoric sea,
And the big rain comes dancing to the earth!
And now again 'tis black,—and now, the glee
Of the loud hills shakes with its mountain-mirth,
As if they did rejoice o'er a young earthquake's birth.

XCIV

Now, where the swift Rhone cleaves his way between
Heights which appear as lovers who have parted
In hate, whose mining depths so intervene,
That they can meet no more, though broken-hearted;
Though in their souls, which thus each other thwarted,
Love was the very root of the fond rage
Which blighted their life's bloom, and then departed:
Itself expired, but leaving them an age
Of years all winters—war within themselves to wage.

XCV

Now, where the quick Rhone thus hath cleft his way,
The mightiest of the storms hath ta'en his stand;
For here, not one, but many, make their play,
And fling their thunderbolts from hand to hand,
Flashing and cast around: of all the band,
The brightest through these parted hills hath forked
His lightnings, as if he did understand
That in such gaps as desolation worked,
There the hot shaft should blast whatever therein lurked.

XCVI

Sky, mountains, river, winds, lake, lightnings! ye,
With night, and clouds, and thunder, and a soul
To make these felt and feeling, well may be
Things that have made me watchful; the far roll
Of your departing voices, is the knoll
Of what in me is sleepless,—if I rest.
But where of ye, O tempests! is the goal?
Are ye like those within the human breast?
Or do ye find at length, like eagles, some high nest?

XCVII

Could I embody and unbosom now
That which is most within me,—could I wreak
My thoughts upon expression, and thus throw
Soul, heart, mind, passions, feelings, strong or weak,
All that I would have sought, and all I seek,
Bear, know, feel, and yet breathe—into one word,
And that one word were lightning, I would speak;
But as it is, I live and die unheard,
With a most voiceless thought, sheathing it as a sword.

XCVIII

The morn is up again, the dewy morn,
With breath all incense, and with cheek all bloom,
Laughing the clouds away with playful scorn,
And living as if earth contained no tomb,—
And glowing into day: we may resume
The march of our existence: and thus I,
Still on thy shores, fair Leman! may find room
And food for meditation, nor pass by
Much, that may give us pause, if pondered fittingly.

XCIX

Clarens! sweet Clarens! birthplace of deep Love!
Thine air is the young breath of passionate thought;
Thy trees take root in love; the snows above
The very glaciers have his colours caught,
And sunset into rose-hues sees them wrought
By rays which sleep there lovingly: the rocks,
The permanent crags, tell here of Love, who sought
In them a refuge from the worldly shocks,
Which stir and sting the soul with hope that woos, then mocks.

C

Clarens! by heavenly feet thy paths are trod,—
Undying Love's, who here ascends a throne
To which the steps are mountains; where the god
Is a pervading life and light,—so shown
Not on those summits solely, nor alone
In the still cave and forest; o'er the flower
His eye is sparkling, and his breath hath blown,
His soft and summer breath, whose tender power
Passes the strength of storms in their most desolate hour.

CI

All things are here of HIM; from the black pines,
Which are his shade on high, and the loud roar
Of torrents, where he listeneth, to the vines
Which slope his green path downward to the shore,
Where the bowed waters meet him, and adore,
Kissing his feet with murmurs; and the wood,
The covert of old trees, with trunks all hoar,
But light leaves, young as joy, stands where it stood,
Offering to him, and his, a populous solitude.

CII

A populous solitude of bees and birds,
And fairy-formed and many coloured things,
Who worship him with notes more sweet than words,
And innocently open their glad wings,
Fearless and full of life: the gush of springs,
And fall of lofty fountains, and the bend
Of stirring branches, and the bud which brings
The swiftest thought of beauty, here extend,
Mingling, and made by Love, unto one mighty end.

CIII

He who hath loved not, here would learn that lore,
And make his heart a spirit: he who knows
That tender mystery, will love the more,
For this is Love's recess, where vain men's woes,
And the world's waste, have driven him far from those,
For 'tis his nature to advance or die;
He stands not still, but or decays, or grows
Into a boundless blessing, which may vie
With the immortal lights, in its eternity!

CIV

'Twas not for fiction chose Rousseau this spot,
Peopling it with affections; but he found
It was the scene which passion must allot
To the mind's purified beings; 'twas the ground
Where early Love his Psyche's zone unbound,
And hallowed it with loveliness: 'tis lone,
And wonderful, and deep, and hath a sound,
And sense, and sight of sweetness; here the Rhone
Hath spread himself a couch, the Alps have reared a throne.

CV

Lausanne! and Ferney! ye have been the abodes
Of names which unto you bequeathed a name;
Mortals, who sought and found, by dangerous roads,
A path to perpetuity of fame:
They were gigantic minds, and their steep aim
Was, Titan-like, on daring doubts to pile
Thoughts which should call down thunder, and the flame
Of Heaven, again assailed, if Heaven the while
On man and man's research could deign do more than smile.

CVI

The one was fire and fickleness, a child
Most mutable in wishes, but in mind
A wit as various,—gay, grave, sage, or wild,—
Historian, bard, philosopher combined:
He multiplied himself among mankind,
The Proteus of their talents: But his own
Breathed most in ridicule,—which, as the wind,
Blew where it listed, laying all things prone,—
Now to o'erthrow a fool, and now to shake a throne.

CVII

The other, deep and slow, exhausting thought,
And hiving wisdom with each studious year,
In meditation dwelt, with learning wrought,
And shaped his weapon with an edge severe,
Sapping a solemn creed with solemn sneer;
The lord of irony,—that master spell,
Which stung his foes to wrath, which grew from fear,
And doomed him to the zealot's ready hell,
Which answers to all doubts so eloquently well.

CVIII

Yet, peace be with their ashes,—for by them,
If merited, the penalty is paid;
It is not ours to judge, far less condemn;
The hour must come when such things shall be made
Known unto all,—or hope and dread allayed
By slumber on one pillow, in the dust,
Which, thus much we are sure, must lie decayed;
And when it shall revive, as is our trust,
'Twill be to be forgiven, or suffer what is just.

CIX

But let me quit man's works, again to read
His Maker's spread around me, and suspend
This page, which from my reveries I feed,
Until it seems prolonging without end.
The clouds above me to the white Alps tend,
And I must pierce them, and survey whate'er
May be permitted, as my steps I bend
To their most great and growing region, where
The earth to her embrace compels the powers of air.

CX

Italia! too, Italia! looking on thee
Full flashes on the soul the light of ages,
Since the fierce Carthaginian almost won thee,
To the last halo of the chiefs and sages
Who glorify thy consecrated pages;
Thou wert the throne and grave of empires; still,
The fount at which the panting mind assuages
Her thirst of knowledge, quaffing there her fill,
Flows from the eternal source of Rome's imperial hill.

CXI

Thus far have I proceeded in a theme
Renewed with no kind auspices:—to feel
We are not what we have been, and to deem
We are not what we should be, and to steel
The heart against itself; and to conceal,
With a proud caution, love or hate, or aught,—
Passion or feeling, purpose, grief, or zeal,—
Which is the tyrant spirit of our thought,
Is a stern task of soul:—No matter,—it is taught.

CXII

And for these words, thus woven into song,
It may be that they are a harmless wile,—
The colouring of the scenes which fleet along,
Which I would seize, in passing, to beguile
My breast, or that of others, for a while.
Fame is the thirst of youth,—but I am not
So young as to regard men's frown or smile
As loss or guerdon of a glorious lot;
I stood and stand alone,—remembered or forgot.

CXIII

I have not loved the world, nor the world me;
I have not flattered its rank breath, nor bowed
To its idolatries a patient knee,—
Nor coined my cheek to smiles, nor cried aloud
In worship of an echo; in the crowd
They could not deem me one of such; I stood
Among them, but not of them; in a shroud
Of thoughts which were not their thoughts, and still could,
Had I not filed my mind, which thus itself subdued.

CXIV

I have not loved the world, nor the world me,—
But let us part fair foes; I do believe,
Though I have found them not, that there may be
Words which are things,—hopes which will not deceive,
And virtues which are merciful, nor weave
Snares for the falling: I would also deem
O'er others' griefs that some sincerely grieve;
That two, or one, are almost what they seem,—
That goodness is no name, and happiness no dream.

CXV

My daughter! with thy name this song begun—
My daughter! with thy name this much shall end—
I see thee not, I hear thee not,—but none
Can be so wrapt in thee; thou art the friend
To whom the shadows of far years extend:
Albeit my brow thou never shouldst behold,
My voice shall with thy future visions blend,
And reach into thy heart, when mine is cold,—
A token and a tone, even from thy father's mould.

CXVI

To aid thy mind's development,—to watch
Thy dawn of little joys,—to sit and see
Almost thy very growth,—to view thee catch
Knowledge of objects, wonders yet to thee!
To hold thee lightly on a gentle knee,
And print on thy soft cheek a parent's kiss,—
This, it should seem, was not reserved for me
Yet this was in my nature:—As it is,
I know not what is there, yet something like to this.

CXVII

Yet, though dull Hate as duty should be taught,
I know that thou wilt love me; though my name
Should be shut from thee, as a spell still fraught
With desolation, and a broken claim:
Though the grave closed between us,—'twere the same,
I know that thou wilt love me: though to drain
My blood from out thy being were an aim,
And an attainment,—all would be in vain,—
Still thou wouldst love me, still that more than life retain.

CXVIII

The child of love,—though born in bitterness,
And nurtured in convulsion. Of thy sire
These were the elements, and thine no less.
As yet such are around thee; but thy fire
Shall be more tempered, and thy hope far higher.
Sweet be thy cradled slumbers! O'er the sea,
And from the mountains where I now respire,
Fain would I waft such blessing upon thee,
As, with a sigh, I deem thou mightst have been to me!

Canto the Fourth

I

I stood in Venice, on the Bridge of Sighs;
A palace and a prison on each hand:
I saw from out the wave her structures rise
As from the stroke of the enchanter's wand:
A thousand years their cloudy wings expand
Around me, and a dying glory smiles
O'er the far times when many a subject land
Looked to the winged Lion's marble piles,
Where Venice sate in state, throned on her hundred isles!

II

She looks a sea Cybele, fresh from ocean,
Rising with her tiara of proud towers
At airy distance, with majestic motion,
A ruler of the waters and their powers:
And such she was; her daughters had their dowers
From spoils of nations, and the exhaustless East
Poured in her lap all gems in sparkling showers.
In purple was she robed, and of her feast
Monarchs partook, and deemed their dignity increased.

III

In Venice, Tasso's echoes are no more,
And silent rows the songless gondolier;
Her palaces are crumbling to the shore,
And music meets not always now the ear:
Those days are gone—but beauty still is here.
States fall, arts fade—but Nature doth not die,
Nor yet forget how Venice once was dear,
The pleasant place of all festivity,
The revel of the earth, the masque of Italy!

IV

But unto us she hath a spell beyond
Her name in story, and her long array
Of mighty shadows, whose dim forms despond
Above the dogeless city's vanished sway;
Ours is a trophy which will not decay
With the Rialto; Shylock and the Moor,
And Pierre, cannot be swept or worn away—
The keystones of the arch! though all were o'er,
For us repeopled were the solitary shore.

V

The beings of the mind are not of clay;
Essentially immortal, they create
And multiply in us a brighter ray
And more beloved existence: that which Fate
Prohibits to dull life, in this our state
Of mortal bondage, by these spirits supplied,
First exiles, then replaces what we hate;
Watering the heart whose early flowers have died,
And with a fresher growth replenishing the void.

VI

Such is the refuge of our youth and age,
The first from Hope, the last from Vacancy;
And this worn feeling peoples many a page,
And, may be, that which grows beneath mine eye:
Yet there are things whose strong reality
Outshines our fairy-land; in shape and hues
More beautiful than our fantastic sky,
And the strange constellations which the Muse
O'er her wild universe is skilful to diffuse:

VII

I saw or dreamed of such,—but let them go—
They came like truth, and disappeared like dreams;
And whatsoe'er they were—are now but so;
I could replace them if I would: still teems
My mind with many a form which aptly seems
Such as I sought for, and at moments found;
Let these too go—for waking reason deems
Such overweening phantasies unsound,
And other voices speak, and other sights surround.

VIII

I've taught me other tongues, and in strange eyes
Have made me not a stranger; to the mind
Which is itself, no changes bring surprise;
Nor is it harsh to make, nor hard to find
A country with—ay, or without mankind;
Yet was I born where men are proud to be,
Not without cause; and should I leave behind
The inviolate island of the sage and free,
And seek me out a home by a remoter sea,

IX

Perhaps I loved it well: and should I lay
My ashes in a soil which is not mine,
My spirit shall resume it—if we may
Unbodied choose a sanctuary. I twine
My hopes of being remembered in my line
With my land's language: if too fond and far
These aspirations in their scope incline,—
If my fame should be, as my fortunes are,
Of hasty growth and blight, and dull Oblivion bar.

X

My name from out the temple where the dead
Are honoured by the nations—let it be—
And light the laurels on a loftier head!
And be the Spartan's epitaph on me—
'Sparta hath many a worthier son than he.'
Meantime I seek no sympathies, nor need;
The thorns which I have reaped are of the tree
I planted,—they have torn me, and I bleed:
I should have known what fruit would spring from such a seed.

XI

The spouseless Adriatic mourns her lord;
And, annual marriage now no more renewed,
The Bucentaur lies rotting unrestored,
Neglected garment of her widowhood!
St. Mark yet sees his lion where he stood
Stand, but in mockery of his withered power,
Over the proud place where an Emperor sued,
And monarchs gazed and envied in the hour
When Venice was a queen with an unequalled dower.

XII

The Suabian sued, and now the Austrian reigns—
An Emperor tramples where an Emperor knelt;
Kingdoms are shrunk to provinces, and chains
Clank over sceptred cities; nations melt
From power's high pinnacle, when they have felt
The sunshine for a while, and downward go
Like lauwine loosened from the mountain's belt:
Oh for one hour of blind old Dandolo!
The octogenarian chief, Byzantium's conquering foe.

XIII

Before St. Mark still glow his steeds of brass,
Their gilded collars glittering in the sun;
But is not Doria's menace come to pass?
Are they not Bridled?—Venice, lost and won,
Her thirteen hundred years of freedom done,
Sinks, like a seaweed, into whence she rose!
Better be whelmed beneath the waves, and shun,
Even in Destruction's depth, her foreign foes,
From whom submission wrings an infamous repose.

XIV

In youth she was all glory,—a new Tyre,—
Her very byword sprung from victory,
The 'Planter of the Lion,' which through fire
And blood she bore o'er subject earth and sea;
Though making many slaves, herself still free
And Europe's bulwark 'gainst the Ottomite:
Witness Troy's rival, Candia! Vouch it, ye
Immortal waves that saw Lepanto's fight!
For ye are names no time nor tyranny can blight.

XV

Statues of glass—all shivered—the long file
Of her dead doges are declined to dust;
But where they dwelt, the vast and sumptuous pile
Bespeaks the pageant of their splendid trust;
Their sceptre broken, and their sword in rust,
Have yielded to the stranger: empty halls,
Thin streets, and foreign aspects, such as must
Too oft remind her who and what enthrals,
Have flung a desolate cloud o'er Venice' lovely walls.

XVI

When Athens' armies fell at Syracuse,
And fettered thousands bore the yoke of war,
Redemption rose up in the Attic Muse,
Her voice their only ransom from afar:
See! as they chant the tragic hymn, the car
Of the o'ermastered victor stops, the reins
Fall from his hands—his idle scimitar
Starts from its belt—he rends his captive's chains,
And bids him thank the bard for freedom and his strains.

XVII

Thus, Venice, if no stronger claim were thine,
Were all thy proud historic deeds forgot,
Thy choral memory of the bard divine,
Thy love of Tasso, should have cut the knot
Which ties thee to thy tyrants; and thy lot
Is shameful to the nations,—most of all,
Albion! to thee: the Ocean Queen should not
Abandon Ocean's children; in the fall
Of Venice think of thine, despite thy watery wall.

XVIII

I loved her from my boyhood: she to me
Was as a fairy city of the heart,
Rising like water-columns from the sea,
Of joy the sojourn, and of wealth the mart
And Otway, Radcliffe, Schiller, Shakspeare's art,
Had stamped her image in me, and e'en so,
Although I found her thus, we did not part,
Perchance e'en dearer in her day of woe,
Than when she was a boast, a marvel, and a show.

XIX

I can repeople with the past—and of
The present there is still for eye and thought,
And meditation chastened down, enough;
And more, it may be, than I hoped or sought;
And of the happiest moments which were wrought
Within the web of my existence, some
From thee, fair Venice! have their colours caught:
There are some feelings Time cannot benumb,
Nor torture shake, or mine would now be cold and dumb.

XX

But from their nature will the tannen grow
Loftiest on loftiest and least sheltered rocks,
Rooted in barrenness, where nought below
Of soil supports them 'gainst the Alpine shocks
Of eddying storms; yet springs the trunk, and mocks
The howling tempest, till its height and frame
Are worthy of the mountains from whose blocks
Of bleak, grey granite, into life it came,
And grew a giant tree;—the mind may grow the same.

XXI

Existence may be borne, and the deep root
Of life and sufferance make its firm abode
In bare and desolate bosoms: mute
The camel labours with the heaviest load,
And the wolf dies in silence. Not bestowed
In vain should such examples be; if they,
Things of ignoble or of savage mood,
Endure and shrink not, we of nobler clay
May temper it to bear,—it is but for a day.

XXII

All suffering doth destroy, or is destroyed,
Even by the sufferer; and, in each event,
Ends:—Some, with hope replenished and rebuoyed,
Return to whence they came—with like intent,
And weave their web again; some, bowed and bent,
Wax grey and ghastly, withering ere their time,
And perish with the reed on which they leant;
Some seek devotion, toil, war, good or crime,
According as their souls were formed to sink or climb.

XXIII

But ever and anon of griefs subdued
There comes a token like a scorpion's sting,
Scarce seen, but with fresh bitterness imbued;
And slight withal may be the things which bring
Back on the heart the weight which it would fling
Aside for ever: it may be a sound—
A tone of music—summer's eve—or spring—
A flower—the wind—the ocean—which shall wound,
Striking the electric chain wherewith we are darkly bound.

XXIV

And how and why we know not, nor can trace
Home to its cloud this lightning of the mind,
But feel the shock renewed, nor can efface
The blight and blackening which it leaves behind,
Which out of things familiar, undesigned,
When least we deem of such, calls up to view
The spectres whom no exorcism can bind,—
The cold—the changed—perchance the dead—anew,
The mourned, the loved, the lost—too many!—yet how few!

XXV

But my soul wanders; I demand it back
To meditate amongst decay, and stand
A ruin amidst ruins; there to track
Fall'n states and buried greatness, o'er a land
Which Was the mightiest in its old command,
And Is the loveliest, and must ever be
The master-mould of Nature's heavenly hand,
Wherein were cast the heroic and the free,
The beautiful, the brave—the lords of earth and sea.

XXVI

The commonwealth of kings, the men of Rome!
And even since, and now, fair Italy!
Thou art the garden of the world, the home
Of all Art yields, and Nature can decree;
Even in thy desert, what is like to thee?
Thy very weeds are beautiful, thy waste
More rich than other climes' fertility;
Thy wreck a glory, and thy ruin graced
With an immaculate charm which cannot be defaced.

XXVII

The moon is up, and yet it is not night—
Sunset divides the sky with her—a sea
Of glory streams along the Alpine height
Of blue Friuli's mountains; Heaven is free
From clouds, but of all colours seems to be—
Melted to one vast Iris of the West,
Where the day joins the past eternity;
While, on the other hand, meek Dian's crest
Floats through the azure air—an island of the blest!

XXVIII

A single star is at her side, and reigns
With her o'er half the lovely heaven; but still
Yon sunny sea heaves brightly, and remains
Rolled o'er the peak of the far Rhaetian hill,
As Day and Night contending were, until
Nature reclaimed her order:—gently flows
The deep-dyed Brenta, where their hues instil
The odorous purple of a new-born rose,
Which streams upon her stream, and glassed within it glows,

XXIX

Filled with the face of heaven, which, from afar,
Comes down upon the waters; all its hues,
From the rich sunset to the rising star,
Their magical variety diffuse:
And now they change; a paler shadow strews
Its mantle o'er the mountains; parting day
Dies like the dolphin, whom each pang imbues
With a new colour as it gasps away,
The last still loveliest, till—'tis gone—and all is grey.

XXX

There is a tomb in Arqua;—reared in air,
Pillared in their sarcophagus, repose
The bones of Laura's lover: here repair
Many familiar with his well-sung woes,
The pilgrims of his genius. He arose
To raise a language, and his land reclaim
From the dull yoke of her barbaric foes:
Watering the tree which bears his lady's name
With his melodious tears, he gave himself to fame.

LORD BYRON

XXXI

They keep his dust in Arqua, where he died;
The mountain-village where his latter days
Went down the vale of years; and 'tis their pride—
An honest pride—and let it be their praise,
To offer to the passing stranger's gaze
His mansion and his sepulchre; both plain
And venerably simple, such as raise
A feeling more accordant with his strain,
Than if a pyramid formed his monumental fane.

XXXII

And the soft quiet hamlet where he dwelt
Is one of that complexion which seems made
For those who their mortality have felt,
And sought a refuge from their hopes decayed
In the deep umbrage of a green hill's shade,
Which shows a distant prospect far away
Of busy cities, now in vain displayed,
For they can lure no further; and the ray
Of a bright sun can make sufficient holiday.

XXXIII

Developing the mountains, leaves, and flowers
And shining in the brawling brook, where-by,
Clear as its current, glide the sauntering hours
With a calm languor, which, though to the eye
Idlesse it seem, hath its morality,
If from society we learn to live,
'Tis solitude should teach us how to die;
It hath no flatterers; vanity can give
No hollow aid; alone—man with his God must strive:

XXXIV

Or, it may be, with demons, who impair
The strength of better thoughts, and seek their prey
In melancholy bosoms, such as were
Of moody texture from their earliest day,
And loved to dwell in darkness and dismay,
Deeming themselves predestined to a doom
Which is not of the pangs that pass away;
Making the sun like blood, the earth a tomb,
The tomb a hell, and hell itself a murkier gloom.

XXXV

Ferrara! in thy wide and grass-grown streets,
Whose symmetry was not for solitude,
There seems as 'twere a curse upon the seat's
Of former sovereigns, and the antique brood
Of Este, which for many an age made good
Its strength within thy walls, and was of yore
Patron or tyrant, as the changing mood
Of petty power impelled, of those who wore
The wreath which Dante's brow alone had worn before.

XXXVI

And Tasso is their glory and their shame.
Hark to his strain! and then survey his cell!
And see how dearly earned Torquato's fame,
And where Alfonso bade his poet dwell.
The miserable despot could not quell
The insulted mind he sought to quench, and blend
With the surrounding maniacs, in the hell
Where he had plunged it. Glory without end
Scattered the clouds away—and on that name attend

XXXVII

The tears and praises of all time, while thine
Would rot in its oblivion—in the sink
Of worthless dust, which from thy boasted line
Is shaken into nothing; but the link
Thou formest in his fortunes bids us think
Of thy poor malice, naming thee with scorn—
Alfonso! how thy ducal pageants shrink
From thee! if in another station born,
Scarce fit to be the slave of him thou mad'st to mourn:

XXXVIII

Thou! formed to eat, and be despised, and die,
Even as the beasts that perish, save that thou
Hadst a more splendid trough, and wider sty:
He! with a glory round his furrowed brow,
Which emanated then, and dazzles now
In face of all his foes, the Cruscan quire,
And Boileau, whose rash envy could allow
No strain which shamed his country's creaking lyre,
That whetstone of the teeth—monotony in wire!

XXXIX

Peace to Torquato's injured shade! 'twas his
In life and death to be the mark where Wrong
Aimed with their poisoned arrows—but to miss.
Oh, victor unsurpassed in modern song!
Each year brings forth its millions; but how long
The tide of generations shall roll on,
And not the whole combined and countless throng
Compose a mind like thine? Though all in one
Condensed their scattered rays, they would not form a sun.

XL

Great as thou art, yet paralleled by those
Thy countrymen, before thee born to shine,
The bards of Hell and Chivalry: first rose
The Tuscan father's comedy divine;
Then, not unequal to the Florentine,
The Southern Scott, the minstrel who called forth
A new creation with his magic line,
And, like the Ariosto of the North,
Sang ladye-love and war, romance and knightly worth.

XLI

The lightning rent from Ariosto's bust
The iron crown of laurel's mimicked leaves;
Nor was the ominous element unjust,
For the true laurel-wreath which Glory weaves
Is of the tree no bolt of thunder cleaves,
And the false semblance but disgraced his brow;
Yet still, if fondly Superstition grieves,
Know that the lightning sanctifies below
Whate'er it strikes;—yon head is doubly sacred now.

XLII

Italia! O Italia! thou who hast
The fatal gift of beauty, which became
A funeral dower of present woes and past,
On thy sweet brow is sorrow ploughed by shame,
And annals graved in characters of flame.
Oh God! that thou wert in thy nakedness
Less lovely or more powerful, and couldst claim
Thy right, and awe the robbers back, who press
To shed thy blood, and drink the tears of thy distress;

LORD BYRON

XLIII

Then mightst thou more appal; or, less desired,
Be homely and be peaceful, undeplored
For thy destructive charms; then, still untired,
Would not be seen the armed torrents poured
Down the deep Alps; nor would the hostile horde
Of many-nationed spoilers from the Po
Quaff blood and water; nor the stranger's sword
Be thy sad weapon of defence, and so,
Victor or vanquished, thou the slave of friend or foe.

XLIV

Wandering in youth, I traced the path of him,
The Roman friend of Rome's least mortal mind,
The friend of Tully: as my bark did skim
The bright blue waters with a fanning wind,
Came Megara before me, and behind
Ægina lay, Piraeus on the right,
And Corinth on the left; I lay reclined
Along the prow, and saw all these unite
In ruin, even as he had seen the desolate sight;

XLV

For time hath not rebuilt them, but upreared
Barbaric dwellings on their shattered site,
Which only make more mourned and more endeared
The few last rays of their far-scattered light,
And the crushed relics of their vanished might.
The Roman saw these tombs in his own age,
These sepulchres of cities, which excite
Sad wonder, and his yet surviving page
The moral lesson bears, drawn from such pilgrimage.

XLVI

That page is now before me, and on mine
His country's ruin added to the mass
Of perished states he mourned in their decline,
And I in desolation: all that Was
Of then destruction Is; and now, alas!
Rome—Rome imperial, bows her to the storm,
In the same dust and blackness, and we pass
The skeleton of her Titanic form,
Wrecks of another world, whose ashes still are warm.

XLVII

Yet, Italy! through every other land
Thy wrongs should ring, and shall, from side to side;
Mother of Arts! as once of Arms; thy hand
Was then our Guardian, and is still our guide;
Parent of our religion! whom the wide
Nations have knelt to for the keys of heaven!
Europe, repentant of her parricide,
Shall yet redeem thee, and, all backward driven,
Roll the barbarian tide, and sue to be forgiven.

XLVIII

But Arno wins us to the fair white walls,
Where the Etrurian Athens claims and keeps
A softer feeling for her fairy halls.
Girt by her theatre of hills, she reaps
Her corn, and wine, and oil, and Plenty leaps
To laughing life, with her redundant horn.
Along the banks where smiling Arno sweeps,
Was modern Luxury of Commerce born,
And buried Learning rose, redeemed to a new morn.

XLIX

There, too, the goddess loves in stone, and fills
The air around with beauty; we inhale
The ambrosial aspect, which, beheld, instils
Part of its immortality; the veil
Of heaven is half undrawn; within the pale
We stand, and in that form and face behold
What Mind can make, when Nature's self would fail;
And to the fond idolaters of old
Envy the innate flash which such a soul could mould:

L

We gaze and turn away, and know not where,
Dazzled and drunk with beauty, till the heart
Reels with its fulness; there—for ever there—
Chained to the chariot of triumphal Art,
We stand as captives, and would not depart.
Away!—there need no words, nor terms precise,
The paltry jargon of the marble mart,
Where Pedantry gulls Folly—we have eyes:
Blood, pulse, and breast, confirm the Dardan Shepherd's prize.

LI

Appearedst thou not to Paris in this guise?
Or to more deeply blest Anchises? or,
In all thy perfect goddess-ship, when lies
Before thee thy own vanquished Lord of War?
And gazing in thy face as toward a star,
Laid on thy lap, his eyes to thee upturn,
Feeding on thy sweet cheek! while thy lips are
With lava kisses melting while they burn,
Showered on his eyelids, brow, and mouth, as from an urn!

LII

Glowing, and circumfused in speechless love,
Their full divinity inadequate
That feeling to express, or to improve,
The gods become as mortals, and man's fate
Has moments like their brightest! but the weight
Of earth recoils upon us;—let it go!
We can recall such visions, and create
From what has been, or might be, things which grow,
Into thy statue's form, and look like gods below.

LIII

I leave to learned fingers, and wise hands,
The artist and his ape, to teach and tell
How well his connoisseurship understands
The graceful bend, and the voluptuous swell:
Let these describe the undescribable:
I would not their vile breath should crisp the stream
Wherein that image shall for ever dwell;
The unruffled mirror of the loveliest dream
That ever left the sky on the deep soul to beam.

LIV

In Santa Croce's holy precincts lie
Ashes which make it holier, dust which is
E'en in itself an immortality,
Though there were nothing save the past, and this
The particle of those sublimities
Which have relapsed to chaos:—here repose
Angelo's, Alfieri's bones, and his,
The starry Galileo, with his woes;
Here Machiavelli's earth returned to whence it rose.

LV

These are four minds, which, like the elements,
Might furnish forth creation:—Italy!
Time, which hath wronged thee with ten thousand rents
Of thine imperial garment, shall deny,
And hath denied, to every other sky,
Spirits which soar from ruin:—thy decay
Is still impregnate with divinity,
Which gilds it with revivifying ray;
Such as the great of yore, Canova is to-day.

LVI

But where repose the all Etruscan three—
Dante, and Petrarch, and, scarce less than they,
The Bard of Prose, creative spirit! he
Of the Hundred Tales of love—where did they lay
Their bones, distinguished from our common clay
In death as life? Are they resolved to dust,
And have their country's marbles nought to say?
Could not her quarries furnish forth one bust?
Did they not to her breast their filial earth entrust?

LVII

Ungrateful Florence! Dante sleeps afar,
Like Scipio, buried by the upbraiding shore;
Thy factions, in their worse than civil war,
Proscribed the bard whose name for evermore
Their children's children would in vain adore
With the remorse of ages; and the crown
Which Petrarch's laureate brow supremely wore,
Upon a far and foreign soil had grown,
His life, his fame, his grave, though rifled—not thine own.

LVIII

Boccaccio to his parent earth bequeathed
His dust,—and lies it not her great among,
With many a sweet and solemn requiem breathed
O'er him who formed the Tuscan's siren tongue?
That music in itself, whose sounds are song,
The poetry of speech? No;—even his tomb
Uptorn, must bear the hyaena bigots' wrong,
No more amidst the meaner dead find room,
Nor claim a passing sigh, because it told for WHOM?

LIX

And Santa Croce wants their mighty dust;
Yet for this want more noted, as of yore
The Caesar's pageant, shorn of Brutus' bust,
Did but of Rome's best son remind her more:
Happier Ravenna! on thy hoary shore,
Fortress of falling empire! honoured sleeps
The immortal exile;—Arqua, too, her store
Of tuneful relics proudly claims and keeps,
While Florence vainly begs her banished dead, and weeps.

LX

What is her pyramid of precious stones?
Of porphyry, jasper, agate, and all hues
Of gem and marble, to encrust the bones
Of merchant-dukes? the momentary dews
Which, sparkling to the twilight stars, infuse
Freshness in the green turf that wraps the dead,
Whose names are mausoleums of the Muse,
Are gently prest with far more reverent tread
Than ever paced the slab which paves the princely head.

LORD BYRON

LXI

There be more things to greet the heart and eyes
In Arno's dome of Art's most princely shrine,
Where Sculpture with her rainbow sister vies;
There be more marvels yet—but not for mine;
For I have been accustomed to entwine
My thoughts with Nature rather in the fields
Than Art in galleries: though a work divine
Calls for my spirit's homage, yet it yields
Less than it feels, because the weapon which it wields

LXII

Is of another temper, and I roam
By Thrasimene's lake, in the defiles
Fatal to Roman rashness, more at home;
For there the Carthaginian's warlike wiles
Come back before me, as his skill beguiles
The host between the mountains and the shore,
Where Courage falls in her despairing files,
And torrents, swoll'n to rivers with their gore,
Reek through the sultry plain, with legions scattered o'er,

LXIII

Like to a forest felled by mountain winds;
And such the storm of battle on this day,
And such the frenzy, whose convulsion blinds
To all save carnage, that, beneath the fray,
An earthquake reeled unheededly away!
None felt stern Nature rocking at his feet,
And yawning forth a grave for those who lay
Upon their bucklers for a winding-sheet;
Such is the absorbing hate when warring nations meet.

LXIV

The Earth to them was as a rolling bark
Which bore them to Eternity; they saw
The Ocean round, but had no time to mark
The motions of their vessel: Nature's law,
In them suspended, recked not of the awe
Which reigns when mountains tremble, and the birds
Plunge in the clouds for refuge, and withdraw
From their down-toppling nests; and bellowing herds
Stumble o'er heaving plains, and man's dread hath no words.

LXV

Far other scene is Thrasimene now;
Her lake a sheet of silver, and her plain
Rent by no ravage save the gentle plough;
Her aged trees rise thick as once the slain
Lay where their roots are; but a brook hath ta'en—
A little rill of scanty stream and bed—
A name of blood from that day's sanguine rain;
And Sanguinetto tells ye where the dead
Made the earth wet, and turned the unwilling waters red.

LXVI

But thou, Clitumnus! in thy sweetest wave
Of the most living crystal that was e'er
The haunt of river nymph, to gaze and lave
Her limbs where nothing hid them, thou dost rear
Thy grassy banks whereon the milk-white steer
Grazes; the purest god of gentle waters!
And most serene of aspect, and most clear:
Surely that stream was unprofaned by slaughters,
A mirror and a bath for Beauty's youngest daughters!

LXVII

And on thy happy shore a temple still,
Of small and delicate proportion, keeps,
Upon a mild declivity of hill,
Its memory of thee; beneath it sweeps
Thy current's calmness; oft from out it leaps
The finny darter with the glittering scales,
Who dwells and revels in thy glassy deeps;
While, chance, some scattered water-lily sails
Down where the shallower wave still tells its bubbling tales.

LXVIII

Pass not unblest the genius of the place!
If through the air a zephyr more serene
Win to the brow, 'tis his; and if ye trace
Along his margin a more eloquent green,
If on the heart the freshness of the scene
Sprinkle its coolness, and from the dry dust
Of weary life a moment lave it clean
With Nature's baptism,—'tis to him ye must
Pay orisons for this suspension of disgust.

LXIX

The roar of waters!—from the headlong height
Velino cleaves the wave-worn precipice;
The fall of waters! rapid as the light
The flashing mass foams shaking the abyss;
The hell of waters! where they howl and hiss,
And boil in endless torture; while the sweat
Of their great agony, wrung out from this
Their Phlegethon, curls round the rocks of jet
That gird the gulf around, in pitiless horror set,

LXX

And mounts in spray the skies, and thence again
Returns in an unceasing shower, which round,
With its unemptied cloud of gentle rain,
Is an eternal April to the ground,
Making it all one emerald. How profound
The gulf! and how the giant element
From rock to rock leaps with delirious bound,
Crushing the cliffs, which, downward worn and rent
With his fierce footsteps, yield in chasms a fearful vent

LXXI

To the broad column which rolls on, and shows
More like the fountain of an infant sea
Torn from the womb of mountains by the throes
Of a new world, than only thus to be
Parent of rivers, which flow gushingly,
With many windings through the vale:—Look back!
Lo! where it comes like an eternity,
As if to sweep down all things in its track,
Charming the eye with dread,—a matchless cataract,

LXXII

Horribly beautiful! but on the verge,
From side to side, beneath the glittering morn,
An Iris sits, amidst the infernal surge,
Like Hope upon a deathbed, and, unworn
Its steady dyes, while all around is torn
By the distracted waters, bears serene
Its brilliant hues with all their beams unshorn:
Resembling, mid the torture of the scene,
Love watching Madness with unalterable mien.

LXXIII

Once more upon the woody Apennine,
    The infant Alps, which—had I not before
Gazed on their mightier parents, where the pine
    Sits on more shaggy summits, and where roar
The thundering lauwine—might be worshipped more;
    But I have seen the soaring Jungfrau rear
Her never-trodden snow, and seen the hoar
    Glaciers of bleak Mont Blanc both far and near,
And in Chimari heard the thunder-hills of fear,

LXXIV

The Acroceraunian mountains of old name;
    And on Parnassus seen the eagles fly
Like spirits of the spot, as 'twere for fame,
    For still they soared unutterably high:
I've looked on Ida with a Trojan's eye;
    Athos, Olympus, Ætna, Atlas, made
These hills seem things of lesser dignity,
    All, save the lone Soracte's height displayed,
Not Now in snow, which asks the lyric Roman's aid

LXXV

For our remembrance, and from out the plain
    Heaves like a long-swept wave about to break,
And on the curl hangs pausing: not in vain
    May he who will his recollections rake,
And quote in classic raptures, and awake
    The hills with Latian echoes; I abhorred
Too much, to conquer for the poet's sake,
    The drilled dull lesson, forced down word by word
In my repugnant youth, with pleasure to record

LXXVI

Aught that recalls the daily drug which turned
My sickening memory; and, though Time hath taught
My mind to meditate what then it learned,
Yet such the fixed inveteracy wrought
By the impatience of my early thought,
That, with the freshness wearing out before
My mind could relish what it might have sought,
If free to choose, I cannot now restore
Its health; but what it then detested, still abhor.

LXXVII

Then farewell, Horace; whom I hated so,
Not for thy faults, but mine; it is a curse
To understand, not feel, thy lyric flow,
To comprehend, but never love thy verse,
Although no deeper moralist rehearse
Our little life, nor bard prescribe his art,
Nor livelier satirist the conscience pierce,
Awakening without wounding the touched heart,
Yet fare thee well—upon Soracte's ridge we part.

LXXVIII

O Rome! my country! city of the soul!
The orphans of the heart must turn to thee,
Lone mother of dead empires! and control
In their shut breasts their petty misery.
What are our woes and sufferance? Come and see
The cypress, hear the owl, and plod your way
O'er steps of broken thrones and temples, Ye!
Whose agonies are evils of a day—
A world is at our feet as fragile as our clay.

LXXIX

The Niobe of nations! there she stands,
  Childless and crownless, in her voiceless woe;
An empty urn within her withered hands,
  Whose holy dust was scattered long ago;
The Scipios' tomb contains no ashes now;
  The very sepulchres lie tenantless
  Of their heroic dwellers: dost thou flow,
Old Tiber! through a marble wilderness?
Rise, with thy yellow waves, and mantle her distress!

LXXX

The Goth, the Christian, Time, War, Flood, and Fire,
  Have dwelt upon the seven-hilled city's pride:
She saw her glories star by star expire,
  And up the steep barbarian monarchs ride,
Where the car climbed the Capitol; far and wide
  Temple and tower went down, nor left a site;—
  Chaos of ruins! who shall trace the void,
O'er the dim fragments cast a lunar light,
And say, 'Here was, or is,' where all is doubly night?

LXXXI

The double night of ages, and of her,
  Night's daughter, Ignorance, hath wrapt, and wrap
All round us; we but feel our way to err:
  The ocean hath its chart, the stars their map;
And knowledge spreads them on her ample lap;
  But Rome is as the desert, where we steer
  Stumbling o'er recollections: now we clap
Our hands, and cry, 'Eureka!' it is clear—
When but some false mirage of ruin rises near.

LXXXII

Alas, the lofty city! and alas
The trebly hundred triumphs! and the day
When Brutus made the dagger's edge surpass
The conqueror's sword in bearing fame away!
Alas for Tully's voice, and Virgil's lay,
And Livy's pictured page! But these shall be
Her resurrection; all beside—decay.
Alas for Earth, for never shall we see
That brightness in her eye she bore when Rome was free!

LXXXIII

O thou, whose chariot rolled on Fortune's wheel,
Triumphant Sylla! Thou, who didst subdue
Thy country's foes ere thou wouldst pause to feel
The wrath of thy own wrongs, or reap the due
Of hoarded vengeance till thine eagles flew
O'er prostrate Asia;—thou, who with thy frown
Annihilated senates—Roman, too,
With all thy vices, for thou didst lay down
With an atoning smile a more than earthly crown—

LXXXIV

The dictatorial wreath,—couldst thou divine
To what would one day dwindle that which made
Thee more than mortal? and that so supine
By aught than Romans Rome should thus be laid?
She who was named eternal, and arrayed
Her warriors but to conquer—she who veiled
Earth with her haughty shadow, and displayed
Until the o'er-canopied horizon failed,
Her rushing wings—Oh! she who was almighty hailed!

LXXXV

Sylla was first of victors; but our own,
The sagest of usurpers, Cromwell!—he
Too swept off senates while he hewed the throne
Down to a block—immortal rebel! See
What crimes it costs to be a moment free
And famous through all ages! But beneath
His fate the moral lurks of destiny;
His day of double victory and death
Beheld him win two realms, and, happier, yield his breath.

LXXXVI

The third of the same moon whose former course
Had all but crowned him, on the self-same day
Deposed him gently from his throne of force,
And laid him with the earth's preceding clay.
And showed not Fortune thus how fame and sway,
And all we deem delightful, and consume
Our souls to compass through each arduous way,
Are in her eyes less happy than the tomb?
Were they but so in man's, how different were his doom!

LXXXVII

And thou, dread statue! yet existent in
The austerest form of naked majesty,
Thou who beheldest, mid the assassins' din,
At thy bathed base the bloody Caesar lie,
Folding his robe in dying dignity,
An offering to thine altar from the queen
Of gods and men, great Nemesis! did he die,
And thou, too, perish, Pompey? have ye been
Victors of countless kings, or puppets of a scene?

LXXXVIII

And thou, the thunder-stricken nurse of Rome!
She-wolf! whose brazen-imaged dugs impart
The milk of conquest yet within the dome
Where, as a monument of antique art,
Thou standest:—Mother of the mighty heart,
Which the great founder sucked from thy wild teat,
Scorched by the Roman Jove's ethereal dart,
And thy limbs blacked with lightning—dost thou yet
Guard thine immortal cubs, nor thy fond charge forget?

LXXXIX

Thou dost;—but all thy foster-babes are dead—
The men of iron; and the world hath reared
Cities from out their sepulchres: men bled
In imitation of the things they feared,
And fought and conquered, and the same course steered,
At apish distance; but as yet none have,
Nor could, the same supremacy have neared,
Save one vain man, who is not in the grave,
But, vanquished by himself, to his own slaves a slave,

XC

The fool of false dominion—and a kind
Of bastard Caesar, following him of old
With steps unequal; for the Roman's mind
Was modelled in a less terrestrial mould,
With passions fiercer, yet a judgment cold,
And an immortal instinct which redeemed
The frailties of a heart so soft, yet bold.
Alcides with the distaff now he seemed
At Cleopatra's feet, and now himself he beamed.

LORD BYRON

XCI

And came, and saw, and conquered. But the man
Who would have tamed his eagles down to flee,
Like a trained falcon, in the Gallic van,
Which he, in sooth, long led to victory,
With a deaf heart which never seemed to be
A listener to itself, was strangely framed;
With but one weakest weakness—vanity:
Coquettish in ambition, still he aimed
At what? Can he avouch, or answer what he claimed?

XCII

And would be all or nothing—nor could wait
For the sure grave to level him; few years
Had fixed him with the Caesars in his fate,
On whom we tread: For THIS the conqueror rears
The arch of triumph! and for this the tears
And blood of earth flow on as they have flowed,
An universal deluge, which appears
Without an ark for wretched man's abode,
And ebbs but to reflow!—Renew thy rainbow, God!

XCIII

What from this barren being do we reap?
Our senses narrow, and our reason frail,
Life short, and truth a gem which loves the deep,
And all things weighed in custom's falsest scale;
Opinion an omnipotence, whose veil
Mantles the earth with darkness, until right
And wrong are accidents, and men grow pale
Lest their own judgments should become too bright,
And their free thoughts be crimes, and earth have too much light.

XCIV

And thus they plod in sluggish misery,
Rotting from sire to son, and age to age,
Proud of their trampled nature, and so die,
Bequeathing their hereditary rage
To the new race of inborn slaves, who wage
War for their chains, and rather than be free,
Bleed gladiator-like, and still engage
Within the same arena where they see
Their fellows fall before, like leaves of the same tree.

XCV

I speak not of men's creeds—they rest between
Man and his Maker—but of things allowed,
Averred, and known,—and daily, hourly seen—
The yoke that is upon us doubly bowed,
And the intent of tyranny avowed,
The edict of Earth's rulers, who are grown
The apes of him who humbled once the proud,
And shook them from their slumbers on the throne;
Too glorious, were this all his mighty arm had done.

XCVI

Can tyrants but by tyrants conquered be,
And Freedom find no champion and no child
Such as Columbia saw arise when she
Sprung forth a Pallas, armed and undefiled?
Or must such minds be nourished in the wild,
Deep in the unpruned forest, midst the roar
Of cataracts, where nursing nature smiled
On infant Washington? Has Earth no more
Such seeds within her breast, or Europe no such shore?

XCVII

But France got drunk with blood to vomit crime,
And fatal have her Saturnalia been
To Freedom's cause, in every age and clime;
Because the deadly days which we have seen,
And vile Ambition, that built up between
Man and his hopes an adamantine wall,
And the base pageant last upon the scene,
Are grown the pretext for the eternal thrall
Which nips Life's tree, and dooms man's worst—his second fall.

XCVIII

Yet, Freedom! yet thy banner, torn, but flying,
Streams like the thunder-storm AGAINST the wind;
Thy trumpet-voice, though broken now and dying,
The loudest still the tempest leaves behind;
Thy tree hath lost its blossoms, and the rind,
Chopped by the axe, looks rough and little worth,
But the sap lasts,—and still the seed we find
Sown deep, even in the bosom of the North;
So shall a better spring less bitter fruit bring forth.

XCIX

There is a stern round tower of other days,
Firm as a fortress, with its fence of stone,
Such as an army's baffled strength delays,
Standing with half its battlements alone,
And with two thousand years of ivy grown,
The garland of eternity, where wave
The green leaves over all by time o'erthrown:
What was this tower of strength? within its cave
What treasure lay so locked, so hid?—A woman's grave.

C

But who was she, the lady of the dead,
  Tombed in a palace? Was she chaste and fair?
  Worthy a king's—or more—a Roman's bed?
  What race of chiefs and heroes did she bear?
  What daughter of her beauties was the heir?
  How lived—how loved—how died she? Was she not
  So honoured—and conspicuously there,
  Where meaner relics must not dare to rot,
Placed to commemorate a more than mortal lot?

CI

Was she as those who love their lords, or they
  Who love the lords of others? such have been
  Even in the olden time, Rome's annals say.
  Was she a matron of Cornelia's mien,
  Or the light air of Egypt's graceful queen,
  Profuse of joy; or 'gainst it did she war,
  Inveterate in virtue? Did she lean
  To the soft side of the heart, or wisely bar
Love from amongst her griefs?—for such the affections are.

CII

Perchance she died in youth: it may be, bowed
  With woes far heavier than the ponderous tomb
  That weighed upon her gentle dust, a cloud
  Might gather o'er her beauty, and a gloom
  In her dark eye, prophetic of the doom
  Heaven gives its favourites—early death; yet shed
  A sunset charm around her, and illume
  With hectic light, the Hesperus of the dead,
Of her consuming cheek the autumnal leaf-like red.

CIII

Perchance she died in age—surviving all,
Charms, kindred, children—with the silver grey
On her long tresses, which might yet recall,
It may be, still a something of the day
When they were braided, and her proud array
And lovely form were envied, praised, and eyed
By Rome—But whither would Conjecture stray?
Thus much alone we know—Metella died,
The wealthiest Roman's wife: Behold his love or pride!

CIV

I know not why—but standing thus by thee
It seems as if I had thine inmate known,
Thou Tomb! and other days come back on me
With recollected music, though the tone
Is changed and solemn, like the cloudy groan
Of dying thunder on the distant wind;
Yet could I seat me by this ivied stone
Till I had bodied forth the heated mind,
Forms from the floating wreck which ruin leaves behind;

CV

And from the planks, far shattered o'er the rocks,
Built me a little bark of hope, once more
To battle with the ocean and the shocks
Of the loud breakers, and the ceaseless roar
Which rushes on the solitary shore
Where all lies foundered that was ever dear:
But could I gather from the wave-worn store
Enough for my rude boat, where should I steer?
There woos no home, nor hope, nor life, save what is here.

CVI

Then let the winds howl on! their harmony
Shall henceforth be my music, and the night
The sound shall temper with the owlet's cry,
As I now hear them, in the fading light
Dim o'er the bird of darkness' native site,
Answer each other on the Palatine,
With their large eyes, all glistening grey and bright,
And sailing pinions.—Upon such a shrine
What are our petty griefs?—let me not number mine.

CVII

Cypress and ivy, weed and wallflower grown
Matted and massed together, hillocks heaped
On what were chambers, arch crushed, column strown
In fragments, choked-up vaults, and frescoes steeped
In subterranean damps, where the owl peeped,
Deeming it midnight:—Temples, baths, or halls?
Pronounce who can; for all that Learning reaped
From her research hath been, that these are walls—
Behold the Imperial Mount! 'tis thus the mighty falls.

CVIII

There is the moral of all human tales:
'Tis but the same rehearsal of the past,
First Freedom, and then Glory—when that fails,
Wealth, vice, corruption—barbarism at last.
And History, with all her volumes vast,
Hath but ONE page,—'tis better written here,
Where gorgeous Tyranny hath thus amassed
All treasures, all delights, that eye or ear,
Heart, soul could seek, tongue ask—Away with words! draw near,

CIX

Admire, exult—despise—laugh, weep—for here
There is such matter for all feeling:—Man!
Thou pendulum betwixt a smile and tear,
Ages and realms are crowded in this span,
This mountain, whose obliterated plan
The pyramid of empires pinnacled,
Of Glory's gewgaws shining in the van
Till the sun's rays with added flame were filled!
Where are its golden roofs? where those who dared to build?

CX

Tully was not so eloquent as thou,
Thou nameless column with the buried base!
What are the laurels of the Caesar's brow?
Crown me with ivy from his dwelling-place.
Whose arch or pillar meets me in the face,
Titus or Trajan's? No; 'tis that of Time:
Triumph, arch, pillar, all he doth displace,
Scoffing; and apostolic statues climb
To crush the imperial urn, whose ashes slept sublime,

CXI

Buried in air, the deep blue sky of Rome,
And looking to the stars; they had contained
A spirit which with these would find a home,
The last of those who o'er the whole earth reigned,
The Roman globe, for after none sustained
But yielded back his conquests:—he was more
Than a mere Alexander, and unstained
With household blood and wine, serenely wore
His sovereign virtues—still we Trajan's name adore.

CXII

Where is the rock of Triumph, the high place
Where Rome embraced her heroes? where the steep
Tarpeian—fittest goal of Treason's race,
The promontory whence the traitor's leap
Cured all ambition? Did the Conquerors heap
Their spoils here? Yes; and in yon field below,
A thousand years of silenced factions sleep—
The Forum, where the immortal accents glow,
And still the eloquent air breathes—burns with Cicero!

CXIII

The field of freedom, faction, fame, and blood:
Here a proud people's passions were exhaled,
From the first hour of empire in the bud
To that when further worlds to conquer failed;
But long before had Freedom's face been veiled,
And Anarchy assumed her attributes:
Till every lawless soldier who assailed
Trod on the trembling Senate's slavish mutes,
Or raised the venal voice of baser prostitutes.

CXIV

Then turn we to our latest tribune's name,
From her ten thousand tyrants turn to thee,
Redeemer of dark centuries of shame—
The friend of Petrarch—hope of Italy—
Rienzi! last of Romans! While the tree
Of freedom's withered trunk puts forth a leaf,
Even for thy tomb a garland let it be—
The forum's champion, and the people's chief—
Her new-born Numa thou, with reign, alas! too brief.

CXV

Egeria! sweet creation of some heart
Which found no mortal resting-place so fair
As thine ideal breast; whate'er thou art
Or wert,—a young Aurora of the air,
The nympholepsy of some fond despair;
Or, it might be, a beauty of the earth,
Who found a more than common votary there
Too much adoring; whatsoe'er thy birth,
Thou wert a beautiful thought, and softly bodied forth.

CXVI

The mosses of thy fountain still are sprinkled
With thine Elysian water-drops; the face
Of thy cave-guarded spring, with years unwrinkled,
Reflects the meek-eyed genius of the place,
Whose green wild margin now no more erase
Art's works; nor must the delicate waters sleep,
Prisoned in marble, bubbling from the base
Of the cleft statue, with a gentle leap
The rill runs o'er, and round, fern, flowers, and ivy creep,

CXVII

Fantastically tangled; the green hills
Are clothed with early blossoms, through the grass
The quick-eyed lizard rustles, and the bills
Of summer birds sing welcome as ye pass;
Flowers fresh in hue, and many in their class,
Implore the pausing step, and with their dyes
Dance in the soft breeze in a fairy mass;
The sweetness of the violet's deep blue eyes,
Kissed by the breath of heaven, seems coloured by its skies.

CXVIII

Here didst thou dwell, in this enchanted cover,
Egeria! thy all heavenly bosom beating
For the far footsteps of thy mortal lover;
The purple Midnight veiled that mystic meeting
With her most starry canopy, and seating
Thyself by thine adorer, what befell?
This cave was surely shaped out for the greeting
Of an enamoured Goddess, and the cell
Haunted by holy Love—the earliest oracle!

CXIX

And didst thou not, thy breast to his replying,
Blend a celestial with a human heart;
And Love, which dies as it was born, in sighing,
Share with immortal transports? could thine art
Make them indeed immortal, and impart
The purity of heaven to earthly joys,
Expel the venom and not blunt the dart—
The dull satiety which all destroys—
And root from out the soul the deadly weed which cloys?

CXX

Alas! our young affections run to waste,
Or water but the desert: whence arise
But weeds of dark luxuriance, tares of haste,
Rank at the core, though tempting to the eyes,
Flowers whose wild odours breathe but agonies,
And trees whose gums are poison; such the plants
Which spring beneath her steps as Passion flies
O'er the world's wilderness, and vainly pants
For some celestial fruit forbidden to our wants.

CXXI

O Love! no habitant of earth thou art—
An unseen seraph, we believe in thee,—
A faith whose martyrs are the broken heart,
But never yet hath seen, nor e'er shall see,
The naked eye, thy form, as it should be;
The mind hath made thee, as it peopled heaven,
Even with its own desiring phantasy,
And to a thought such shape and image given,
As haunts the unquenched soul—parched—wearied—wrung—and riven.

CXXII

Of its own beauty is the mind diseased,
And fevers into false creation;—where,
Where are the forms the sculptor's soul hath seized?
In him alone. Can Nature show so fair?
Where are the charms and virtues which we dare
Conceive in boyhood and pursue as men,
The unreached Paradise of our despair,
Which o'er-informs the pencil and the pen,
And overpowers the page where it would bloom again.

CXXIII

Who loves, raves—'tis youth's frenzy—but the cure
Is bitterer still; as charm by charm unwinds
Which robed our idols, and we see too sure
Nor worth nor beauty dwells from out the mind's
Ideal shape of such; yet still it binds
The fatal spell, and still it draws us on,
Reaping the whirlwind from the oft-sown winds;
The stubborn heart, its alchemy begun,
Seems ever near the prize—wealthiest when most undone.

CXXIV

We wither from our youth, we gasp away—
Sick—sick; unfound the boon, unslaked the thirst,
Though to the last, in verge of our decay,
Some phantom lures, such as we sought at first—
But all too late,—so are we doubly curst.
Love, fame, ambition, avarice—'tis the same—
Each idle, and all ill, and none the worst—
For all are meteors with a different name,
And death the sable smoke where vanishes the flame.

CXXV

Few—none—find what they love or could have loved:
Though accident, blind contact, and the strong
Necessity of loving, have removed
Antipathies—but to recur, ere long,
Envenomed with irrevocable wrong;
And Circumstance, that unspiritual god
And miscreator, makes and helps along
Our coming evils with a crutch-like rod,
Whose touch turns hope to dust—the dust we all have trod.

CXXVI

Our life is a false nature—'tis not in
The harmony of things,—this hard decree,
This uneradicable taint of sin,
This boundless upas, this all-blasting tree,
Whose root is earth, whose leaves and branches be
The skies which rain their plagues on men like dew—
Disease, death, bondage, all the woes we see—
And worse, the woes we see not—which throb through
The immedicable soul, with heart-aches ever new.

CXXVII

Yet let us ponder boldly—'tis a base
Abandonment of reason to resign
Our right of thought—our last and only place
Of refuge; this, at least, shall still be mine:
Though from our birth the faculty divine
Is chained and tortured—cabined, cribbed, confined,
And bred in darkness, lest the truth should shine
Too brightly on the unprepared mind,
The beam pours in, for time and skill will couch the blind.

CXXVIII

Arches on arches! as it were that Rome,
Collecting the chief trophies of her line,
Would build up all her triumphs in one dome,
Her Coliseum stands; the moonbeams shine
As 'twere its natural torches, for divine
Should be the light which streams here, to illume
This long explored but still exhaustless mine
Of contemplation; and the azure gloom
Of an Italian night, where the deep skies assume

CXXIX

Hues which have words, and speak to ye of heaven,
Floats o'er this vast and wondrous monument,
And shadows forth its glory. There is given
Unto the things of earth, which Time hath bent,
A spirit's feeling, and where he hath leant
His hand, but broke his scythe, there is a power
And magic in the ruined battlement,
For which the palace of the present hour
Must yield its pomp, and wait till ages are its dower.

CXXX

O Time! the beautifier of the dead,
Adorner of the ruin, comforter
And only healer when the heart hath bled—
Time! the corrector where our judgments err,
The test of truth, love,—sole philosopher,
For all beside are sophists, from thy thrift,
Which never loses though it doth defer—
Time, the avenger! unto thee I lift
My hands, and eyes, and heart, and crave of thee a gift:

CXXXI

Amidst this wreck, where thou hast made a shrine
And temple more divinely desolate,
Among thy mightier offerings here are mine,
Ruins of years—though few, yet full of fate:
If thou hast ever seen me too elate,
Hear me not; but if calmly I have borne
Good, and reserved my pride against the hate
Which shall not whelm me, let me not have worn
This iron in my soul in vain—shall THEY not mourn?

CXXXII

And thou, who never yet of human wrong
Left the unbalanced scale, great Nemesis!
Here, where the ancients paid thee homage long—
Thou, who didst call the Furies from the abyss,
And round Orestes bade them howl and hiss
For that unnatural retribution—just,
Had it but been from hands less near—in this
Thy former realm, I call thee from the dust!
Dost thou not hear my heart?—Awake! thou shalt, and must.

CXXXIII

It is not that I may not have incurred
For my ancestral faults or mine the wound
I bleed withal, and had it been conferred
With a just weapon, it had flowed unbound.
But now my blood shall not sink in the ground;
To thee I do devote it—THOU shalt take
The vengeance, which shall yet be sought and found,
Which if *I* have not taken for the sake—
But let that pass—I sleep, but thou shalt yet awake.

CXXXIV

And if my voice break forth, 'tis not that now
I shrink from what is suffered: let him speak
Who hath beheld decline upon my brow,
Or seen my mind's convulsion leave it weak;
But in this page a record will I seek.
Not in the air shall these my words disperse,
Though I be ashes; a far hour shall wreak
The deep prophetic fulness of this verse,
And pile on human heads the mountain of my curse!

CXXXV

That curse shall be forgiveness.—Have I not—
Hear me, my mother Earth! behold it, Heaven!—
Have I not had to wrestle with my lot?
Have I not suffered things to be forgiven?
Have I not had my brain seared, my heart riven,
Hopes sapped, name blighted, Life's life lied away?
And only not to desperation driven,
Because not altogether of such clay
As rots into the souls of those whom I survey.

CXXXVI

From mighty wrongs to petty perfidy
Have I not seen what human things could do?
From the loud roar of foaming calumny
To the small whisper of the as paltry few
And subtler venom of the reptile crew,
The Janus glance of whose significant eye,
Learning to lie with silence, would SEEM true,
And without utterance, save the shrug or sigh,
Deal round to happy fools its speechless obloquy.

CXXXVII

But I have lived, and have not lived in vain:
My mind may lose its force, my blood its fire,
And my frame perish even in conquering pain,
But there is that within me which shall tire
Torture and Time, and breathe when I expire:
Something unearthly, which they deem not of,
Like the remembered tone of a mute lyre,
Shall on their softened spirits sink, and move
In hearts all rocky now the late remorse of love.

CXXXVIII

The seal is set.—Now welcome, thou dread Power
Nameless, yet thus omnipotent, which here
Walk'st in the shadow of the midnight hour
With a deep awe, yet all distinct from fear:
Thy haunts are ever where the dead walls rear
Their ivy mantles, and the solemn scene
Derives from thee a sense so deep and clear
That we become a part of what has been,
And grow unto the spot, all-seeing but unseen.

CXXXIX

And here the buzz of eager nations ran,
In murmured pity, or loud-roared applause,
As man was slaughtered by his fellow-man.
And wherefore slaughtered? wherefore, but because
Such were the bloody circus' genial laws,
And the imperial pleasure.—Wherefore not?
What matters where we fall to fill the maws
Of worms—on battle-plains or listed spot?
Both are but theatres where the chief actors rot.

CXL

I see before me the Gladiator lie:
He leans upon his hand—his manly brow
Consents to death, but conquers agony,
And his drooped head sinks gradually low—
And through his side the last drops, ebbing slow
From the red gash, fall heavy, one by one,
Like the first of a thunder-shower; and now
The arena swims around him: he is gone,
Ere ceased the inhuman shout which hailed the wretch who won.

CXLI

He heard it, but he heeded not—his eyes
Were with his heart, and that was far away;
He recked not of the life he lost nor prize,
But where his rude hut by the Danube lay,
THERE were his young barbarians all at play,
THERE was their Dacian mother—he, their sire,
Butchered to make a Roman holiday—
All this rushed with his blood—Shall he expire,
And unavenged?—Arise! ye Goths, and glut your ire!

CXLII

But here, where murder breathed her bloody steam;
And here, where buzzing nations choked the ways,
And roared or murmured like a mountain-stream
Dashing or winding as its torrent strays;
Here, where the Roman million's blame or praise
Was death or life, the playthings of a crowd,
My voice sounds much—and fall the stars' faint rays
On the arena void—seats crushed, walls bowed,
And galleries, where my steps seem echoes strangely loud.

CXLIII

A ruin—yet what ruin! from its mass
Walls, palaces, half-cities, have been reared;
Yet oft the enormous skeleton ye pass,
And marvel where the spoil could have appeared.
Hath it indeed been plundered, or but cleared?
Alas! developed, opens the decay,
When the colossal fabric's form is neared:
It will not bear the brightness of the day,
Which streams too much on all, years, man, have reft away.

CXLIV

But when the rising moon begins to climb
Its topmost arch, and gently pauses there;
When the stars twinkle through the loops of time,
And the low night-breeze waves along the air,
The garland-forest, which the grey walls wear,
Like laurels on the bald first Caesar's head;
When the light shines serene, but doth not glare,
Then in this magic circle raise the dead:
Heroes have trod this spot—'tis on their dust ye tread.

CXLV

'While stands the Coliseum, Rome shall stand;
When falls the Coliseum, Rome shall fall;
And when Rome falls—the World.' From our own land
Thus spake the pilgrims o'er this mighty wall
In Saxon times, which we are wont to call
Ancient; and these three mortal things are still
On their foundations, and unaltered all;
Rome and her Ruin past Redemption's skill,
The World, the same wide den—of thieves, or what ye will.

CXLVI

Simple, erect, severe, austere, sublime—
Shrine of all saints and temple of all gods,
From Jove to Jesus—spared and blest by time;
Looking tranquillity, while falls or nods
Arch, empire, each thing round thee, and man plods
His way through thorns to ashes—glorious dome!
Shalt thou not last?—Time's scythe and tyrants' rods
Shiver upon thee—sanctuary and home
Of art and piety—Pantheon!—pride of Rome!

CXLVII

Relic of nobler days, and noblest arts!
Despoiled yet perfect, with thy circle spreads
A holiness appealing to all hearts—
To art a model; and to him who treads
Rome for the sake of ages, Glory sheds
Her light through thy sole aperture; to those
Who worship, here are altars for their beads;
And they who feel for genius may repose
Their eyes on honoured forms, whose busts around them close.

CXLVIII

There is a dungeon, in whose dim drear light
What do I gaze on? Nothing: Look again!
Two forms are slowly shadowed on my sight—
Two insulated phantoms of the brain:
It is not so: I see them full and plain—
An old man, and a female young and fair,
Fresh as a nursing mother, in whose vein
The blood is nectar:—but what doth she there,
With her unmantled neck, and bosom white and bare?

CXLIX

Full swells the deep pure fountain of young life,
Where ON the heart and FROM the heart we took
Our first and sweetest nurture, when the wife,
Blest into mother, in the innocent look,
Or even the piping cry of lips that brook
No pain and small suspense, a joy perceives
Man knows not, when from out its cradled nook
She sees her little bud put forth its leaves—
What may the fruit be yet?—I know not—Cain was Eve's.

CL

But here youth offers to old age the food,
The milk of his own gift:—it is her sire
To whom she renders back the debt of blood
Born with her birth. No; he shall not expire
While in those warm and lovely veins the fire
Of health and holy feeling can provide
Great Nature's Nile, whose deep stream rises higher
Than Egypt's river:—from that gentle side
Drink, drink and live, old man! heaven's realm holds no such tide.

CLI

The starry fable of the milky way
Has not thy story's purity; it is
A constellation of a sweeter ray,
And sacred Nature triumphs more in this
Reverse of her decree, than in the abyss
Where sparkle distant worlds:—Oh, holiest nurse!
No drop of that clear stream its way shall miss
To thy sire's heart, replenishing its source
With life, as our freed souls rejoin the universe.

CLII

Turn to the mole which Hadrian reared on high,
Imperial mimic of old Egypt's piles,
Colossal copyist of deformity,
Whose travelled phantasy from the far Nile's
Enormous model, doomed the artist's toils
To build for giants, and for his vain earth,
His shrunken ashes, raise this dome: How smiles
The gazer's eye with philosophic mirth,
To view the huge design which sprung from such a birth!

CLIII

But lo! the dome—the vast and wondrous dome,
To which Diana's marvel was a cell—
Christ's mighty shrine above his martyr's tomb!
I have beheld the Ephesian's miracle—
Its columns strew the wilderness, and dwell
The hyaena and the jackal in their shade;
I have beheld Sophia's bright roofs swell
Their glittering mass i' the sun, and have surveyed
Its sanctuary the while the usurping Moslem prayed;

CLIV

But thou, of temples old, or altars new,
Standest alone—with nothing like to thee—
Worthiest of God, the holy and the true,
Since Zion's desolation, when that he
Forsook his former city, what could be,
Of earthly structures, in his honour piled,
Of a sublimer aspect? Majesty,
Power, Glory, Strength, and Beauty, all are aisled
In this eternal ark of worship undefiled.

CLV

Enter: its grandeur overwhelms thee not;
And why? it is not lessened; but thy mind,
Expanded by the genius of the spot,
Has grown colossal, and can only find
A fit abode wherein appear enshrined
Thy hopes of immortality; and thou
Shalt one day, if found worthy, so defined,
See thy God face to face, as thou dost now
His Holy of Holies, nor be blasted by his brow.

CLVI

Thou movest—but increasing with th' advance,
Like climbing some great Alp, which still doth rise,
Deceived by its gigantic elegance;
Vastness which grows—but grows to harmonise—
All musical in its immensities;
Rich marbles—richer painting—shrines where flame
The lamps of gold—and haughty dome which vies
In air with Earth's chief structures, though their frame
Sits on the firm-set ground—and this the clouds must claim.

CLVII

Thou seest not all; but piecemeal thou must break
To separate contemplation, the great whole;
And as the ocean many bays will make,
That ask the eye—so here condense thy soul
To more immediate objects, and control
Thy thoughts until thy mind hath got by heart
Its eloquent proportions, and unroll
In mighty graduations, part by part,
The glory which at once upon thee did not dart.

CLVIII

Not by its fault—but thine: Our outward sense
Is but of gradual grasp—and as it is
That what we have of feeling most intense
Outstrips our faint expression; e'en so this
Outshining and o'erwhelming edifice
Fools our fond gaze, and greatest of the great
Defies at first our nature's littleness,
Till, growing with its growth, we thus dilate
Our spirits to the size of that they contemplate.

CLIX

Then pause and be enlightened; there is more
In such a survey than the sating gaze
Of wonder pleased, or awe which would adore
The worship of the place, or the mere praise
Of art and its great masters, who could raise
What former time, nor skill, nor thought could plan;
The fountain of sublimity displays
Its depth, and thence may draw the mind of man
Its golden sands, and learn what great conceptions can.

CLX

Or, turning to the Vatican, go see
Laocoon's torture dignifying pain—
A father's love and mortal's agony
With an immortal's patience blending:—Vain
The struggle; vain, against the coiling strain
And gripe, and deepening of the dragon's grasp,
The old man's clench; the long envenomed chain
Rivets the living links,—the enormous asp
Enforces pang on pang, and stifles gasp on gasp.

CLXI

Or view the Lord of the unerring bow,
The God of life, and poesy, and light—
The Sun in human limbs arrayed, and brow
All radiant from his triumph in the fight;
The shaft hath just been shot—the arrow bright
With an immortal's vengeance; in his eye
And nostril beautiful disdain, and might
And majesty, flash their full lightnings by,
Developing in that one glance the Deity.

CLXII

But in his delicate form—a dream of Love,
Shaped by some solitary nymph, whose breast
Longed for a deathless lover from above,
And maddened in that vision—are expressed
All that ideal beauty ever blessed
The mind within its most unearthly mood,
When each conception was a heavenly guest—
A ray of immortality—and stood
Starlike, around, until they gathered to a god?

CLXIII

And if it be Prometheus stole from heaven
The fire which we endure, it was repaid
By him to whom the energy was given
Which this poetic marble hath arrayed
With an eternal glory—which, if made
By human hands, is not of human thought
And Time himself hath hallowed it, nor laid
One ringlet in the dust—nor hath it caught
A tinge of years, but breathes the flame with which 'twas wrought.

CLXIV

But where is he, the pilgrim of my song,
The being who upheld it through the past?
Methinks he cometh late and tarries long.
He is no more—these breathings are his last;
His wanderings done, his visions ebbing fast,
And he himself as nothing:—if he was
Aught but a phantasy, and could be classed
With forms which live and suffer—let that pass—
His shadow fades away into Destruction's mass,

CLXV

Which gathers shadow, substance, life, and all
That we inherit in its mortal shroud,
And spreads the dim and universal pall
Thro' which all things grow phantoms; and the cloud
Between us sinks and all which ever glowed,
Till Glory's self is twilight, and displays
A melancholy halo scarce allowed
To hover on the verge of darkness; rays
Sadder than saddest night, for they distract the gaze,

CLXVI

And send us prying into the abyss,
  To gather what we shall be when the frame
  Shall be resolved to something less than this
  Its wretched essence; and to dream of fame,
  And wipe the dust from off the idle name
  We never more shall hear,—but never more,
  Oh, happier thought! can we be made the same:
  It is enough, in sooth, that ONCE we bore
These fardels of the heart—the heart whose sweat was gore.

CLXVII

Hark! forth from the abyss a voice proceeds,
  A long, low distant murmur of dread sound,
  Such as arises when a nation bleeds
  With some deep and immedicable wound;
  Through storm and darkness yawns the rending ground.
  The gulf is thick with phantoms, but the chief
  Seems royal still, though with her head discrowned,
  And pale, but lovely, with maternal grief
She clasps a babe, to whom her breast yields no relief.

CLXVIII

Scion of chiefs and monarchs, where art thou?
  Fond hope of many nations, art thou dead?
  Could not the grave forget thee, and lay low
  Some less majestic, less beloved head?
  In the sad midnight, while thy heart still bled,
  The mother of a moment, o'er thy boy,
  Death hushed that pang for ever: with thee fled
  The present happiness and promised joy
Which filled the imperial isles so full it seemed to cloy.

CLXIX

Peasants bring forth in safety.—Can it be,
O thou that wert so happy, so adored!
Those who weep not for kings shall weep for thee,
And Freedom's heart, grown heavy, cease to hoard
Her many griefs for One; for she had poured
Her orisons for thee, and o'er thy head
Beheld her Iris.—Thou, too, lonely lord,
And desolate consort—vainly wert thou wed!
The husband of a year! the father of the dead!

CLXX

Of sackcloth was thy wedding garment made:
Thy bridal's fruit is ashes; in the dust
The fair-haired Daughter of the Isles is laid,
The love of millions! How we did entrust
Futurity to her! and, though it must
Darken above our bones, yet fondly deemed
Our children should obey her child, and blessed
Her and her hoped-for seed, whose promise seemed
Like star to shepherd's eyes; 'twas but a meteor beamed.

CLXXI

Woe unto us, not her; for she sleeps well:
The fickle reek of popular breath, the tongue
Of hollow counsel, the false oracle,
Which from the birth of monarchy hath rung
Its knell in princely ears, till the o'erstrung
Nations have armed in madness, the strange fate
Which tumbles mightiest sovereigns, and hath flung
Against their blind omnipotence a weight
Within the opposing scale, which crushes soon or late,—

CLXXII

These might have been her destiny; but no,
Our hearts deny it: and so young, so fair,
Good without effort, great without a foe;
But now a bride and mother—and now THERE!
How many ties did that stern moment tear!
From thy Sire's to his humblest subject's breast
Is linked the electric chain of that despair,
Whose shock was as an earthquake's, and oppressed
The land which loved thee so, that none could love thee best.

CLXXIII

Lo, Nemi! navelled in the woody hills
So far, that the uprooting wind which tears
The oak from his foundation, and which spills
The ocean o'er its boundary, and bears
Its foam against the skies, reluctant spares
The oval mirror of thy glassy lake;
And, calm as cherished hate, its surface wears
A deep cold settled aspect nought can shake,
All coiled into itself and round, as sleeps the snake.

CLXXIV

And near Albano's scarce divided waves
Shine from a sister valley;—and afar
The Tiber winds, and the broad ocean laves
The Latian coast where sprung the Epic war,
'Arms and the Man,' whose reascending star
Rose o'er an empire,—but beneath thy right
Tully reposed from Rome;—and where yon bar
Of girdling mountains intercepts the sight,
The Sabine farm was tilled, the weary bard's delight.

CLXXV

But I forget.—My pilgrim's shrine is won,
And he and I must part,—so let it be,—
His task and mine alike are nearly done;
Yet once more let us look upon the sea:
The midland ocean breaks on him and me,
And from the Alban mount we now behold
Our friend of youth, that ocean, which when we
Beheld it last by Calpe's rock unfold
Those waves, we followed on till the dark Euxine rolled

CLXXVI

Upon the blue Symplegades: long years—
Long, though not very many—since have done
Their work on both; some suffering and some tears
Have left us nearly where we had begun:
Yet not in vain our mortal race hath run,
We have had our reward—and it is here;
That we can yet feel gladdened by the sun,
And reap from earth, sea, joy almost as dear
As if there were no man to trouble what is clear.

CLXXVII

Oh! that the Desert were my dwelling-place,
With one fair Spirit for my minister,
That I might all forget the human race,
And, hating no one, love but only her!
Ye Elements!—in whose ennobling stir
I feel myself exalted—can ye not
Accord me such a being? Do I err
In deeming such inhabit many a spot?
Though with them to converse can rarely be our lot.

CLXXVIII

There is a pleasure in the pathless woods,
There is a rapture on the lonely shore,
There is society where none intrudes,
By the deep Sea, and music in its roar:
I love not Man the less, but Nature more,
From these our interviews, in which I steal
From all I may be, or have been before,
To mingle with the Universe, and feel
What I can ne'er express, yet cannot all conceal.

CLXXIX

Roll on, thou deep and dark blue Ocean—roll!
Ten thousand fleets sweep over thee in vain;
Man marks the earth with ruin—his control
Stops with the shore;—upon the watery plain
The wrecks are all thy deed, nor doth remain
A shadow of man's ravage, save his own,
When for a moment, like a drop of rain,
He sinks into thy depths with bubbling groan,
Without a grave, unknelled, uncoffined, and unknown.

CLXXX

His steps are not upon thy paths,—thy fields
Are not a spoil for him,—thou dost arise
And shake him from thee; the vile strength he wields
For earth's destruction thou dost all despise,
Spurning him from thy bosom to the skies,
And send'st him, shivering in thy playful spray
And howling, to his gods, where haply lies
His petty hope in some near port or bay,
And dashest him again to earth:—there let him lay.

LORD BYRON

CLXXXI

The armaments which thunderstrike the walls
Of rock-built cities, bidding nations quake,
And monarchs tremble in their capitals.
The oak leviathans, whose huge ribs make
Their clay creator the vain title take
Of lord of thee, and arbiter of war;
These are thy toys, and, as the snowy flake,
They melt into thy yeast of waves, which mar
Alike the Armada's pride, or spoils of Trafalgar.

CLXXXII

Thy shores are empires, changed in all save thee—
Assyria, Greece, Rome, Carthage, what are they?
Thy waters washed them power while they were free
And many a tyrant since: their shores obey
The stranger, slave, or savage; their decay
Has dried up realms to deserts: not so thou,
Unchangeable save to thy wild waves' play—
Time writes no wrinkle on thine azure brow—
Such as creation's dawn beheld, thou rollest now.

CLXXXIII

Thou glorious mirror, where the Almighty's form
Glasses itself in tempests; in all time,
Calm or convulsed—in breeze, or gale, or storm,
Icing the pole, or in the torrid clime
Dark-heaving;—boundless, endless, and sublime—
The image of Eternity—the throne
Of the Invisible; even from out thy slime
The monsters of the deep are made; each zone
Obeys thee: thou goest forth, dread, fathomless, alone.

CLXXXIV

And I have loved thee, Ocean! and my joy
Of youthful sports was on thy breast to be
Borne like thy bubbles, onward: from a boy
I wantoned with thy breakers—they to me
Were a delight; and if the freshening sea
Made them a terror—'twas a pleasing fear,
For I was as it were a child of thee,
And trusted to thy billows far and near,
And laid my hand upon thy mane—as I do here.

CLXXXV

My task is done—my song hath ceased—my theme
Has died into an echo; it is fit
The spell should break of this protracted dream.
The torch shall be extinguished which hath lit
My midnight lamp—and what is writ, is writ—
Would it were worthier! but I am not now
That which I have been—and my visions flit
Less palpably before me—and the glow
Which in my spirit dwelt is fluttering, faint, and low.

CLXXXVI

Farewell! a word that must be, and hath been—
A sound which makes us linger; yet, farewell!
Ye, who have traced the Pilgrim to the scene
Which is his last, if in your memories dwell
A thought which once was his, if on ye swell
A single recollection, not in vain
He wore his sandal-shoon and scallop shell;
Farewell! with Him alone may rest the pain,
If such there were—with YOU, the moral of his strain.

LORD BYRON

A Note About the Author

George Gordon Byron (1788–1824), also known as Lord Byron, was a London-born politician and poet who contributed to the Romantic Movement. He was the son of Captain John Gordon and a wealthy Scottish heiress, Catherine Gordon. Gordon was educated at Trinity College but was more interested in the social scene than his studies. Despite his ambivalence, Gordon was a prolific writer with an affinity for politics. He published his first volume of poetry, *Hours of Idleness* in 1807 and subsequently joined the House of Lords in 1809. Despite his untimely passing at age 36, Gordon led an accomplished life.

A Note from the Publisher

Spanning many genres, from non-fiction essays to literature classics to children's books and lyric poetry, Mint Edition books showcase the master works of our time in a modern new package. The text is freshly typeset, is clean and easy to read, and features a new note about the author in each volume. Many books also include exclusive new introductory material. Every book boasts a striking new cover, which makes it as appropriate for collecting as it is for gift giving. Mint Edition books are only printed when a reader orders them, so natural resources are not wasted. We're proud that our books are never manufactured in excess and exist only in the exact quantity they need to be read and enjoyed.

bookfinity™

Discover more of your favorite classics with Bookfinity™.

- Track your reading with custom book lists.
- Get great book recommendations for your personalized Reader Type.
- Add reviews for your favorite books.
- AND MUCH MORE!

Visit **bookfinity.com** and take the fun Reader Type quiz to get started.

Enjoy our classic and modern companion pairings!

Classic & Modern